AZORES TRAV PORTUGAL GUIDE 2024

Your Ultimate Guide for Insider Tips on Where to Eat, Stay, Play, Exciting Activities, Unlock Secrets, Embrace Paradise, Enjoy Exclusive Local Insights on Dining and Plan Perfect Itineraries

PAMELA JADEN

Copyright © PAMELA JADEN, 2023

All rights reserved

No part of this publication may be reproduced, distributed, or transmitted in any form or by any means, including photocopying, recording, or other electronic or mechanical methods, without the prior written permission of the publisher, except for brief quotations in critical reviews and certain other noncommercial uses permitted by copyright law.

TABLE OF CONTENT

INTRODUCTION
    0.1 Welcome to the Azores
    0.2 About The Azores Archipelago
    0.3 Why Visit the Azores in 2024?

CHAPTER 1
Planning Your Trip
    1.1 Best Time to Visit
    1.2 How to Get to the Azores
By Air
    1.3 Visa and Entry Requirements
    1.4 Currency and Money Matters
    1.5 Travel Insurance
    1.6 Packing Tips
    1.7 Language and Communication
    1.8 Useful Phrases
    1.9 Safety Tips for Travelers

CHAPTER 2
The Islands of Azores
    2.9 Which Islands to Visit and Why

CHAPTER 3
Top Attractions & Activities
    3.2 Outdoor Adventures
    3.3 Cultural and Historical Sites
    3.4 Local Cuisine and Food Experiences

CHAPTER 4
Accommodation Options

4.1 Hotels and Resorts
4.2 Guesthouses and Bed & Breakfasts
4.3 Best Self-Catering Apartments and Villas
4.4 Best Camping and Eco-Lodges

CHAPTER 5
Transportation in the Azores

5.1 Renting a Car: Exploring the Azores at Your Own Pace

5.2 Public Transportation: Navigating the Azores with Ease

5.3 Taxis and Ridesharing: Seamless Mobility in the Azores

CHAPTER 6
Travel Tips for a Memorable Experience

6.2 Sustainable Tourism Practices

6.3 Photography Tips: Capturing Azores' Beauty Through Your Lens

6.4 Unique Souvenirs to Bring Home: Preserving Azorean Memories

CHAPTER 7
Practical Information

7.1 Emergency Contacts: Your Safety Net in the Azores

7.2 Health and Medical Services: Your Well-being in the Azores

7.3 Internet and Connectivity: Staying Connected in the Azores

7.4 Important Local Customs and Etiquette: Navigating Azorean Culture with Respect

CHAPTER 8
Azores Travel Itinerary Suggestions
    8.1 One-Week Itinerary
    8.2 Two-Week Itinerary: A Deep Dive into Azorean Beauty and Culture

Conclusion

Embark on Your Azorean Odyssey

INTRODUCTION

Welcome to the Azores, where nature's beauty thrives in its purest form. As you embark on a journey through these enchanting islands, prepare to be captivated by landscapes that seem plucked from the realms of fantasy. This comprehensive Azores Portugal Travel Guide 2024 is your ticket to discovering a world where emerald-green pastures meet azure crater lakes, and dramatic cliffs embrace the crashing waves.

Picture yourself stepping foot on São Miguel, the largest and most diverse island of the Azores, where lush forests give way to cascading waterfalls and vibrant botanical gardens. Traverse the winding roads that lead to the awe-inspiring Sete Cidades crater lakes, as you bear witness to the harmonious dance of two distinct colors shimmering across the water's surface. Venture into the mystical

Furnas Valley, where geothermal wonders bring about bubbling hot springs and thermal baths, providing an inviting respite for the adventurous traveler. But the allure of the Azores extends beyond São Miguel.

Terceira beckons you with its historic charm, boasting UNESCO-listed Angra do Heroísmo, a living museum of Portuguese colonial heritage. Faial, known as the "Blue Island," invites you to explore the lively port city of Horta, adorned with vibrant murals that recount the tales of intrepid sailors who have crossed the Atlantic.
For those with an affinity for the wild, Pico awaits, with its soaring volcanic peak and fertile vineyards, producing some of Portugal's finest wines. And as the sea sings its siren's song, the islands of São Jorge, Graciosa, Flores, and Corvo stand ready to enthrall you with their unique landscapes and cultural tapestries.The Azores remains an alluring destination for

eco-adventurers and nature enthusiasts alike. Whether you seek adrenaline-pumping experiences like whale-watching or yearn for tranquility amidst unspoiled vistas, the Azores promises to fulfill your every desire. Dive into the crystal-clear waters for a rendezvous with fascinating marine life, or hike through verdant trails that lead to hidden gems awaiting your discovery.

Beyond its natural wonders, the Azores offers a taste of authentic Portuguese culture, where you can savor delectable local dishes, explore charming villages, and immerse yourself in warm, welcoming communities. Discover the Azorean tradition of handicrafts, passed down through generations, and take home a piece of this magical place in the form of a cherished souvenir.

In this guide, we'll equip you with all the essential information to make your Azores adventure seamless and unforgettable. From practical tips on planning your trip and navigating the islands to insightful itineraries that cater to different travel preferences, we've got you covered. Embrace the spirit of sustainable travel as we encourage responsible exploration, ensuring that the magic of the Azores remains preserved for generations to come.

So, embark on this extraordinary journey with us, and let the Azores cast its spell upon you. Let your wanderlust soar amidst landscapes that seem to have been plucked from dreams, and find solace in the embrace of nature's splendor. The Azores awaits your arrival, ready to bestow upon you an experience that will leave an indelible mark on your heart

0.1 Welcome to the Azores

The Azores invites you with open arms, ready to share its magic and leave an indelible mark on your heart. A confidential gem in the vast spectrum of the Atlantic Ocean, where nature's marvels await to captivate your soul and ignite your sense of wonder. As you step foot on this extraordinary archipelago, you will discover a paradise like no other—a place where time slows down, and the boundaries between reality and fantasy blur.

Prepare to be embraced by the warmth of the Azorean spirit, as friendly faces greet you with genuine smiles and open arms. Whether you are a seasoned traveler or embarking on your first adventure, the Azores promises to be an unforgettable journey, where the pure essence of nature remains untouched by the modern world.

From the very moment you arrive, you will be immersed in a tapestry of sights, sounds, and scents that will awaken your senses. Azure crater lakes mirror the ever-changing skies, while volcanic peaks pierce through the clouds, creating an otherworldly panorama that defies description. The lush landscapes, adorned with vibrant flora and fauna, invite you to wander along the countless trails that lead to hidden waterfalls, mystical caves, and secluded coves.

It's not just the landscapes that make the Azores special—it's the harmony between man and nature. Here, tradition and modernity intertwine, as centuries-old practices are preserved and celebrated amidst the embrace of progress. You'll find charming villages, where whitewashed houses with colorful trim stand in contrast to the emerald fields. Friendly locals will share with you their stories, their customs, and their love for the land they call home.

As you explore each island, you'll be enchanted by its unique personality. São Miguel, the "Green Island," welcomes you with its bustling capital, Ponta Delgada, and invites you to unwind in soothing hot springs. Terceira, the "Lilac Island," charms you with its cobblestone streets and UNESCO-listed heritage. Faial, the "Blue Island," captivates you with its maritime history and cosmopolitan vibe.

Dare to go off the beaten path and venture to the lesser-known islands, where untouched beauty awaits your discovery. From the majestic Pico Mountain to the serene Flores waterfalls, every corner of the Azores has a story to tell—a story of resilience, beauty, and of a land that holds its visitors in awe.

Embrace the Azores' sustainable ethos, for here, conservation and preservation are cherished values. Join the movement to protect the unique ecosystems and marine life that thrive in these pristine waters. Let your visit be a testament to the importance of responsible travel, as we strive to ensure that the Azores remains an unspoiled haven for generations to come. We invite you to leave behind the cares of the world and embrace the freedom of exploration. Allow yourself to be mesmerized by the ever-changing landscapes, to be nourished by the local cuisine, and to be moved by the genuine hospitality of the Azorean people.

May your journey through these enchanted islands be filled with unforgettable moments, profound connections, and a renewed appreciation for the beauty of our natural world. Prepare to embark on a voyage of a lifetime—a voyage to the Azores, where dreams become reality, and where the ordinary transforms into the extraordinary.

0.2 About The Azores Archipelago

In the middle of the vast Atlantic Ocean lies a small island paradise that few have had the privilege to visit. The crystal-clear waters, white sandy beaches, and lush tropical vegetation make this hidden gem a true wonder of nature.

The Azores Archipelago is a group of nine volcanic islands that exude a mystical charm and a captivating beauty. Located approximately 1,500 kilometers west of mainland Portugal, this remote destination has long been a well-kept secret among travelers seeking an authentic and unspoiled paradise. Comprising an autonomous region of Portugal, the Azores boast a rich history, diverse landscapes, and a unique cultural heritage that sets them apart as an enchanting corner of the world.

Geographically, the Azores are divided into three distinct groups: **the Eastern Group**, consisting of São Miguel and Santa Maria; **the Central Group**, comprised of Terceira, Graciosa, São Jorge, Pico, and Faial; and **the Western Group**, featuring Flores and Corvo. Each island possesses its distinct character, yet all share a common thread of natural splendor, making the Azores an enticing destination for outdoor enthusiasts and nature lovers alike.

The Azores' volcanic origins have gifted the islands with dramatic topography, featuring soaring peaks, crater lakes, hot springs, and vast plains. The breathtaking landscapes are an outdoor playground, offering a plethora of activities such as hiking, trekking, diving, whale-watching, and birdwatching. Pico Island stands proudly as the highest peak in Portugal, with its eponymous volcano dominating the skyline. The Sete Cidades twin lakes on São

Miguel, with their contrasting blue and green colors, capture the imaginations of all who behold them. Beyond the natural wonders, the Azores bear the marks of a rich cultural tapestry woven over centuries. Influenced by a mix of Portuguese, Azorean, and other international traditions, the islands' culture is a fusion of art, music, festivals, and gastronomy. From the traditional bullfights in Terceira to the vibrant street art in Horta on Faial, each island has its unique expressions of identity and pride.

The Azorean people are renowned for their hospitality, welcoming visitors with open hearts and genuine warmth. The locals take pride in sharing their cultural heritage and folklore with travelers, visiting the Azores an immersive and authentic experience. Time-honored traditions such as the Carnaval and the Festas do Espírito Santo add a sense of festivity and celebration to the islands throughout the year.

As a sanctuary for marine life, the Azores are a haven for wildlife enthusiasts and conservationists. The surrounding ocean teems with an abundance of marine species, including dolphins, sperm whales, blue whales, and even the elusive beaked whales. Responsible whale-watching tours offer an opportunity to witness these majestic creatures in their natural habitat while adhering to strict environmental guidelines.

In recent years, the Azores have become a haven for sustainable tourism, where eco-friendly practices and conservation efforts are actively encouraged. The islands' commitment to preserving their pristine environment and unique biodiversity has garnered recognition worldwide, making the Azores a prime example of how tourism can coexist harmoniously with nature.

In summary, the Azores Archipelago is a realm of unparalleled beauty, a place where landscapes forged by volcanic activity merge with a vibrant cultural heritage and a deep sense of connection to nature. Whether you seek thrilling adventures, cultural exploration, or peaceful seclusion, the Azores beckon with open arms, inviting you to embark on an unforgettable journey of discovery and wonder. Prepare to be enchanted, captivated, and inspired as you uncover the treasures of this extraordinary archipelago in the heart of the Atlantic Ocean.

0.3 Why Visit the Azores in 2024?

1. **Enchanting Nature Unleashed:** Prepare to be bewitched by the Azores' raw and untouched beauty. Embrace landscapes that seem like they were plucked from dreams – from emerald crater lakes to soaring volcanic peaks and lush forests.

2. **Thrill Seekers' Paradise:** Calling all adventure enthusiasts! This is your chance to hike through mystical trails, dive into azure waters teeming with marine life, and witness majestic whales breaching the ocean's surface. The Azores offer an adrenaline-packed playground like no other.
3. **Hidden Gems Await:** Wanderlust will lead you to the lesser-known islands where authentic experiences thrive. Explore charming villages, meet friendly locals, and immerse yourself in rich cultural traditions – stories and memories you'll cherish forever.
4. **Sustainable Heaven:** As sustainable tourism flourishes, the Azores stand as a shining example. Contribute to responsible travel and conservation efforts while indulging in guilt-free exploration. Leave behind only

footprints and take home unforgettable experiences.

5. **Tranquility in Abundance:** In a fast-paced world, the Azores offer a tranquil oasis to rejuvenate your spirit. Relish in serene moments amidst breathtaking vistas, where time seems to stand still, allowing you to disconnect and find inner peace.

6. **Festivals and Fiestas:** Celebrate life as you join locals in vibrant festivals and fiestas that bring the islands to life. Savor the rich tapestry of Azorean culture, from traditional dances to delicious gastronomic delights.

7. **Whale-Watching Extravaganza:** Embark on a once-in-a-lifetime encounter with awe-inspiring marine giants. The Azores' nutrient-rich waters provide the perfect stage for an

unforgettable rendezvous with playful dolphins and magnificent whales.

8. **Unpredictable Beauty:** No two moments in the Azores are the same. Witness ever-changing landscapes that shift with the seasons and weather. Each day is a new canvas of colors, ensuring every visit is truly one-of-a-kind.

9. **Embrace the Azorean Spirit:** Feel the warmth and authenticity of the Azorean people. Their genuine hospitality will make you feel like family, leaving you with cherished memories and a sense of belonging in this remote paradise.

10. **Explore the Unexplored:** Fulfill your wanderlust by venturing off the beaten path. Unveil hidden treasures, secret grottoes, and secluded beaches. Embrace the spirit of discovery as you chart your course through a world waiting to be explored.

11. **Uncrowded:** The Azores are not as crowded as many other popular tourist destinations. You'll be able to enjoy the stunning scenery and activities without the crowds.

12. **Affordability:** The Azores are a relatively affordable travel destination. You can get good deals on flights, accommodation, and activities.

If you're looking for an unforgettable travel experience in 2024, the Azores are the perfect destination for you. With their stunning natural beauty, and warm hospitality, and where adventure, tranquility, sustainability, and rich culture converge in perfect harmony, the Azores are sure to leave you wanting more.

So what are you waiting for? Start preparing your trip to the Azores today! Let this year be the canvas for your most remarkable journey yet—a journey that promises to captivate your heart and soul.

CHAPTER 1

Planning Your Trip

1.1 Best Time to Visit

The Azores boast a temperate maritime climate, making them a year-round destination with each season offering unique experiences. However, certain periods may better align with your preferences and interests. Here's a comprehensive guide to help you choose the best time to visit the Azores:

1. **Spring (March to May):**
    a. **Temperature:** Pleasantly mild, with daytime temperatures ranging from 15°C to 20°C (59°F to 68°F).
    b. **Landscape:** Springtime brings a burst of vibrant colors as flowers bloom, and the countryside

transforms into a picturesque haven.

c. **Activities:** Hiking, exploring gardens, and experiencing the vibrant nature is best during this time. Additionally, spring is an excellent time for birdwatching as migratory birds pass through the islands.

1. **Summer (June to August):**
    - **Temperature:** Warm and pleasant, with daytime temperatures averaging between 20°C to 25°C (68°F to 77°F).
    - **Landscape:** The islands come alive with lush greenery, and the seas offer inviting conditions for water-based activities.
    - **Activities:** Summer is ideal for whale-watching, swimming, diving, and enjoying the coastal

beauty. Festivals and cultural events also flourish during this time.

1. **Fall (September to November):**
   - **Temperature:** Mild temperatures ranging from 15°C to 20°C (59°F to 68°F).
   - **Landscape:** Fall brings a tapestry of warm hues as the foliage starts to change colors.
   - **Activities:** This season offers a quieter atmosphere, making it perfect for nature walks, exploring local culture, and indulging in delicious seasonal foods.

1. **Winter (December to February):**
   - **Temperature:** Still mild, with daytime temperatures around 14°C to 17°C (57°F to 63°F).
   - **Landscape:** The countryside remains lush, and the coastal cliffs showcase their dramatic beauty under the winter sun.
   - **Activities:** While water-based activities are limited, winter is perfect for cozy escapes, soaking in hot springs, and enjoying the peace and tranquility of the islands.

Overall, the best time to visit the Azores largely depends on your preferences. If you enjoy milder temperatures and blossoming landscapes, spring might be the ideal choice. For warmer weather and a vibrant atmosphere, summer is your go-to season. Fall offers a quieter experience with pleasant temperatures, while winter presents a unique charm with its serene ambiance.

Regardless of the time you choose to visit, the Azores are a year-round destination and will welcome you with its enchanting beauty, warm hospitality, and a myriad of activities that promise an unforgettable experience amidst the splendors of nature.

1.2 How to Get to the Azores

By Air

The Azores are located in the middle of the Atlantic Ocean, about 1,500 miles from Portugal. There are a few different airlines that fly to the Azores, including:

- Azores Airlines
- SATA Air Azores
- TAP Portugal

The closest major airport is in Ponta Delgada, on the island of São Miguel. There are also airports on the islands of Faial, Terceira, Pico, and Santa Maria. Once you arrive in Ponta Delgada, you can take a taxi, bus, or ferry to other islands in the Azores. There are also inter-island flights available.

1. **Direct Flights:**
   - **International Flights:** Direct flights to the Azores from major cities in North America and Europe start at approximately $500 to $1000 for economy class, depending on the departure location, season, and booking time.
   - **North America:** Direct flights from Boston and Toronto to the Azores typically range from $500 to $900 for a round-trip ticket in economy class.

- **Europe:** Flights from European cities like Lisbon, Porto, London, Amsterdam, and Frankfurt to the Azores usually start at around $400 to $800 for a round-trip ticket in economy class.

1. **Connecting Flights:**
    - Connecting flights through transit hubs like Lisbon or Porto can be more affordable but may require longer travel times. Connecting flights from North America or Europe to the Azores can start at approximately $350 to $600 for a round-trip ticket in economy class, depending on the layover duration and airline.
    - Airlines like TAP Air Portugal and other major carriers offer connecting flights to the Azores, allowing you to create your

itinerary with convenient layovers.

1. **Inter-Island Flights:**
   - Once in the Azores, inter-island flights on SATA Air Açores start at around $50 to $150 per one-way ticket, depending on the route and island destination.
   - Inter-island flights are relatively short and offer an excellent opportunity to enjoy stunning aerial views of the archipelago.

1. **Total Estimated Price:**
   - The total estimated cost of a round-trip flight to the Azores from North America can range from $850 to $1,500 in economy class, depending on the departure city, season, and booking time.
   - For travelers coming from Europe, the total estimated cost of

a round-trip flight can range from $450 to $1,200 in economy class, depending on the departure city, season, and booking time.

1. **Tips to Find Affordable Flights:**
   - **Book Early:** Flights to the Azores tend to be cheaper when booked well in advance, especially during non-peak travel seasons.
   - **Be Flexible:** If possible, be flexible with your travel dates and consider traveling during shoulder seasons for better deals.
   - **Use Fare Comparison Websites:** Utilize fare comparison websites and flight search engines to compare prices across different airlines and find the best deals.
   - **Sign up for Fare Alerts:** Subscribe to fare alerts and newsletters from airlines or travel

websites to receive notifications about special promotions and discounts.

Please note that the estimated prices mentioned above are subject to change based on various factors, including seasonality, demand, and current travel conditions. It's essential to check real-time prices and availability before making any travel arrangements to the Azores. Additionally, prices can vary significantly depending on the class of service, baggage allowances, and other factors, so it's advisable to review all options when planning your trip.

1.2.2 By Sea

There are a few different ferry companies that sail to the Azores, including:
- Atlanticoline
- Fred Olsen Express
- Lineas Romero.

The ferries typically depart from Lisbon, Portugal, and take about 3 days to reach the Azores. Some ferries depart from the Canary Islands and Madeira.

The estimated price of a one-way ferry ticket to the Azores from Lisbon ranges from \$200 to \$500. The estimated price of a one-way ferry ticket to the Azores from the Canary Islands or Madeira ranges from \$300 to \$700. Once you arrive in the Azores, you can take a taxi, bus, or ferry to other islands in the archipelago.

Here are some other options:
1. **Cruise Ships:**
    - **Cruise Ship Itineraries:** Some cruise lines offer itineraries that include stops in the Azores. Cruising to the Azores provides a unique opportunity to visit multiple islands in one journey,

but the time spent on each island may be limited.
- **Estimated Price:** The cost of a cruise to the Azores can vary widely depending on the cruise line, cabin category, and the length of the itinerary. Prices for a 7-night cruise to the Azores can start at around $800 to $2,000 per person, but luxury or longer cruises may have higher prices.

1. **Ferry Services:**
    - **Ferry Routes:** Regular ferry services operate between some of the islands in the Azores, providing a more leisurely way to explore the archipelago and experience island-hopping.
    - **Estimated Price:** The cost of ferry tickets between islands can vary based on the distance and

route. Prices for one-way ferry tickets can range from $20 to $60 per person, depending on the islands and the type of ferry service.

1. **Transatlantic Voyages:**
   - **Transatlantic Sailings:** Some private sailing vessels and yachts offer transatlantic voyages that may include stops in the Azores as part of their itinerary.
   - **Estimated Price:** The cost of joining a transatlantic sailing voyage can be quite expensive and is highly variable, depending on factors such as the length of the journey, the vessel's amenities, and the level of comfort and service provided.

1. **Estimated Total Price:**
   - The total cost of traveling to the Azores by sea will depend on the chosen method of transport, the type of accommodation (cabin class or stateroom category), the cruise or ferry route, the duration of the journey, and any additional amenities or services included.
1. **Tips to Find Affordable Sea Travel:**
   - **Research and Compare:** Research different cruise lines, ferry companies, and sailing voyages to compare prices, itineraries, and available amenities.
   - **Book in Advance:** Booking well in advance may provide access to early booking discounts and promotions.

- **Be Flexible:** If possible, be flexible with your travel dates to take advantage of special deals or off-peak pricing.

Please note that the estimated prices mentioned above are for reference only and can vary significantly based on factors such as the time of booking, demand, seasonal variations, and specific travel preferences.

Additionally, prices for cruises and ferry services can fluctuate depending on the time of year and other external factors. It is essential to check real-time prices and availability directly with the respective cruise lines, ferry operators, or sailing companies when planning your trip to the Azores by sea.

1.3 Visa and Entry Requirements

Citizens of most countries do not need a visa to enter the Azores for stays of up to 90 days. However, there are a few exceptions, including citizens of countries that do not have visa-free agreements with the European Union.

Here are the entry requirements for the Azores:

1. **Schengen Area:**
   - The Azores, being part of Portugal, are also part of the Schengen Area. If you are a citizen of a country that is part of the Schengen Agreement, you can enter the Azores without a visa for short stays (usually up to 90 days) visit for tourism, business, or family.

1. **Visa-Free Entry:**
   - Citizens of many countries are granted visa-free entry to the Azores for short stays. This includes citizens of the United States, Canada, Australia, New Zealand, the United Kingdom, and most European Union countries, among others.
   - The specific list of countries eligible for visa-free entry may change, so it's essential to check the latest visa requirements before traveling.
1. **Valid Passport:**
   - All travelers, regardless of their nationality, must have a valid passport to enter the Azores. The passport must be valid for at least three months after the proposed stay.

1. **Visa for Non-Schengen Citizens:**
   - If you are a citizen of a country that is not part of the Schengen Area, you may need to apply for a Schengen visa to enter the Azores for short stays. This visa allows you to travel within the Schengen Area, including the Azores, for up to 90 days within 180 days.
   - Schengen visa applications are usually processed by the Portuguese embassy or consulate in your home country or country of residence.
1. **Long-Term Stays and Work Visas:**
   - If you plan to stay in the Azores for longer than 90 days or wish to work or study in the archipelago, you will need to apply for a long-stay visa or a specific work or study visa. These visas have

different requirements and application processes.

1. **Travel Insurance:**
   - While not a visa requirement, having travel insurance is strongly recommended when visiting the Azores. Travel insurance provides coverage for medical emergencies, trip cancellations, lost baggage, and other unforeseen situations, offering peace of mind during your trip.

1. **Entry Requirements for Minors:**
   - If traveling with minors, additional documentation, such as a parental consent letter, may be required. Before traveling, confirm the particular requirements with the embassy or consulate.

1. **Customs and Immigration:**
   - Upon arrival in the Azores, travelers must go through customs and immigration control, where their passports and visa (if applicable) will be checked.
   - **Yellow fever vaccination:** If you are arriving from a country with a risk of yellow fever, you must have a yellow fever vaccination certificate.
   - **Proof of onward travel:** You must have proof of onward travel, such as a plane ticket or a ferry ticket.

It's essential to verify the most up-to-date visa and entry requirements for your specific nationality before planning your trip to the Azores. Visa regulations can change over time, and requirements may vary based on the purpose of your visit and the country you are traveling from. Contact the Portuguese embassy or consulate in your country or visit the official website of the Portuguese immigration authority for the most accurate and current information.

If you are planning to stay in the Azores for longer than 90 days, you will need to apply for a residence permit. You can apply for a residence permit at the Portuguese Immigration and Border Service office in the Azores.

If you are not sure whether you need a visa to enter the Azores, you can check the website of the Portuguese Ministry of Foreign Affairs.

Here are the links to the websites of the Portuguese Ministry of Foreign Affairs and the Portuguese Immigration and Border Service:

- Portuguese Ministry of Foreign Affairs: https://www.mne.gov.pt/
- Portuguese Immigration and Border Service: https://www.sef.pt/

1.4 Currency and Money Matters

The Azores is part of the European Union, so the euro is used throughout the archipelago.

There are ATMs in all major cities and towns in the Azores, so you can easily withdraw cash. You can also use credit cards in most businesses, but it is always a good idea to have some cash on hand, especially if you are traveling to smaller towns or villages.

The exchange rate for the euro is constantly fluctuating, but it is currently around **1 EUR = $1.12**.

1. **Currency:**
    - The Euro (€) is the Azores' official currency. As an autonomous region of Portugal, the Azores use the same currency as the mainland of Portugal and other Eurozone countries.

1. **Cash and Cards:**
   - **Cash:** While credit and debit cards are widely accepted in most places, it's a good idea to carry some cash, especially when visiting more remote areas or smaller establishments where card payments might not be available.
   - **ATMs:** ATMs (Multibanco) are readily available in major towns and cities, providing a convenient way to withdraw cash in Euros using international credit or debit cards.
1. **Currency Exchange:**
   - Currency exchange services are available at airports, major hotels, and some banks. However, exchange rates may not be as favorable as withdrawing cash from an ATM.

- It's advisable to exchange currency in the Azores rather than in your home country to avoid additional fees and get a better rate.

1. **Credit Cards and Payment Methods**
    - **Credit and Debit Cards:** Visa and MasterCard are widely accepted throughout the Azores, especially in larger establishments such as hotels, restaurants, and shops. Some places may also accept American Express and other major credit cards.
    - **Contactless Payments:** Contactless card payments are becoming more common, offering a quick and convenient way to pay for small purchases.

1. **Tipping:**
   - Tipping is not obligatory in the Azores, as service charges are typically included in restaurant bills. However, it's common to leave a small tip as a gesture of appreciation for good service. Rounding up the bill or leaving a few Euros is appreciated but not mandatory.
1. **Prices and Costs:**
   - The cost of living in the Azores is generally lower than in many other European destinations. Prices for accommodation, meals, and activities can vary depending on the island and the level of luxury.
   - Local markets and supermarkets offer an economical way to purchase food and beverages,

allowing you to enjoy delicious local produce without breaking the bank.

1. **Travel Insurance:**
   - While not directly related to currency, it's essential to have travel insurance that covers medical emergencies, trip cancellations, and other unforeseen situations during your trip to the Azores. Confirm that your insurance provides adequate coverage for your specific needs.

1. **VAT Refund:**
   - Tourists visiting the Azores from outside the European Union may be eligible for a Value Added Tax (VAT) refund on certain purchases. Look for shops displaying a "Tax-Free" sticker and follow the necessary

procedures to claim the refund at the airport before departing.

It's always a good idea to inform your bank of your travel plans before visiting the Azores to avoid any potential issues with using your cards abroad. Overall, the Azores offer a range of payment options, making it easy for travelers to manage their money and enjoy the archipelago's beauty and hospitality.

1.5 **Travel Insurance**

Travel insurance is an essential aspect of trip planning to the Azores, providing financial protection and peace of mind during your journey and it covers you for unexpected events that may occur during your trip, such as medical expenses, trip cancellation, and lost luggage. It is important to have travel insurance when you travel to the Azores, as there are many risks that you may be exposed to, such as:

1. **Medical Coverage**
- **Medical Emergencies:** The Azores has a good public healthcare system, but it can be expensive to receive medical treatment there. Ensure your travel insurance covers medical expenses, including hospitalization, emergency medical treatment, doctor's visits, and medical evacuation if necessary. Medical emergencies can be costly, and insurance can help protect you from unexpected expenses.
1. **Trip Cancellation and Interruption:**
    - **Trip Cancellation:** This coverage reimburses non-refundable trip costs if you need to cancel your trip due to unforeseen circumstances, such as illness, injury, or a family emergency.
    - **Trip Interruption:** Covers the costs if you need to cut short your

trip and return home due to covered reasons.

1. **Baggage and Personal Belongings:**
   - **Baggage Loss/Delay:** Offers coverage for lost, stolen, or delayed baggage. This includes reimbursement for essential items you may need to purchase if your baggage is delayed.
   - **Personal Belongings:** Covers loss or damage to personal belongings, such as electronics, cameras, and valuables, during your trip.
1. **Travel Delay and Missed Connections:**
   - **Travel Delay:** Reimburses additional expenses incurred due to flight or travel delays caused by covered reasons, such as bad weather or mechanical issues.

- **Missed Connections:** Covers expenses for rebooking flights or accommodation if you miss a connecting flight due to a covered delay.

1. **Emergency Assistance Services:**
   - **24/7 Emergency Assistance:** Access to a 24-hour helpline for emergency assistance, including medical advice, translation services, and travel information.
   - **Medical Evacuation:** Provides coverage for emergency medical evacuation or repatriation back home if necessary.

When choosing a travel insurance policy for the Azores, it is important to consider the following factors:

1. **Rental Car Coverage (if applicable):**
   - **Rental Car Insurance:** If you plan to rent a car in the Azores,

check if your travel insurance includes coverage for rental car damage or liability.

1. **Adventure Activities:**
   - Check if your travel insurance covers adventure activities such as hiking, diving, and whale-watching, which are popular in the Azores.

1. **Pre-Existing Conditions:**
   - Some travel insurance policies may offer coverage for pre-existing medical conditions if you meet specific criteria. Be sure to review the policy terms and conditions regarding pre-existing conditions.

1. **Policy Limits and Deductibles:**
   - Understand the policy limits, sub-limits, and deductibles of

your travel insurance to ensure they meet your needs.

1. **Read the Policy Document:**
- Before purchasing travel insurance, carefully read the policy document to understand what is covered, any exclusions, and how to make a claim.
- **Premium:** The premium is the amount of money that you will have to pay for the policy. Compare the premiums of different policies to find the best deal.

Remember to choose a reputable insurance provider with good customer service and a track record of handling claims promptly and efficiently. Travel insurance for the Azores will provide you with added security, allowing you to enjoy your trip with confidence, knowing that you are protected against unforeseen events.

1.6 Packing Tips

When packing for the Azores, keep the following in mind

1. **The weather may be erratic:** Because the Azores lie in the Atlantic Ocean, the weather may be erratic. Because it is possible to experience all four seasons in a single day, it is prudent to prepare for a range of weather situations.
2. **There are several outdoor activities available:** Hiking, motorcycling, and whale viewing are all popular outdoor activities in the Azores. As a result, you should pack appropriately.
3. **The Azores are a relaxed vacation destination:** The Azores are a laid-back location, so don't bring anything too extravagant. However, you should bring comfortable clothing that you can move about in.

Here is a list of stuff you should bring with you on your vacation to the Azores:

1. **Clothing for the Weather:** Because the temperature in the Azores is pleasant and unpredictable, bring a combination of lightweight and layered clothes. Include:
- T-shirts
- Shorts
- Light pants
- Skirts
- light jacket or sweater for chilly nights.
- For unexpected rain showers, a waterproof and windproof jacket is important.

1. **comfy Footwear:** Because you will be walking a lot, bring comfy shoes.
- Bring good walking shoes or hiking boots, particularly if you want to enjoy the natural beauty of the islands and hiking paths.

- For beach days and informal excursions, sandals or flip-flops are ideal. Swimwear and beach basics, such as:
- Beach towel,
- Sun hats should not be overlooked.

The beaches and natural swimming holes of the Azores provide wonderful options for leisure and aquatic sports.

1. **Travel Adapters and Charges:** Because the Azores utilize Type F electrical outlets, bring the necessary travel adapters and charges for your electronic equipment.
   - Sunscreen with a high SPF is recommended, since the sun may be intense, particularly during the summer months. Bring:
   - sunglasses
   - broad-brimmed hat for extra sun protection.

1. **Insect Repellent:** While rarely a major concern, mosquitoes, and other insects may be present in certain regions of the Azores. Bring mosquito repellant with you to ensure a pleasant stay. Prescriptions and a basic first-aid kit with necessities such as:
- Bandages
- Painkillers
- Antiseptic creams are recommended. When traveling, it is usually a good idea to include a first-aid kit.
1. **Reusable Water Bottle:** Carry a reusable water bottle with you on your adventures to stay hydrated. Because the tap water in the Azores is safe to drink, you may replenish your bottle at a variety of sites.
- A tiny daypack or backpack is useful for transporting items on day trips and treks.

1. **Camera and Binoculars:** The Azores are a wonderful area, so bring your camera or smartphone to record the breathtaking vistas. Binoculars are also handy for seeing birds and marine life.
- Carry some cash (Euros) with you for little transactions and areas where card payments may not be accepted. Credit and debit cards are generally accepted, but it's a good idea to keep some cash on hand in case of an emergency.
- Bring waterproof bags or pouches to safeguard your devices and other belongings while participating in outdoor activities and boat excursions.
- Keep your passport, travel insurance documentation, and any necessary visas in a secure and immediately accessible location.

1. **Lightweight travel Towel:**

Beach visits and other water activities benefit from a lightweight, quick-drying travel towel.

1. **Respectful Attire:** Dress modestly while visiting churches or religious places to show respect for local traditions.

By following these packing suggestions, you'll be well-prepared to experience the Azores' various landscapes, outdoor activities, and hospitable culture. Remember to pack light and allow room for souvenirs to bring home treasured memories of this magnificent archipelago.

1.7 Language and Communication

When you are planning on visiting the Azores, it is a good idea to learn some basic Portuguese phrases. This will make communicating with locals easier and your vacation more pleasurable.

1. **Official Language:**
   - The official language of the Azores is Portuguese. Portuguese is widely spoken and understood by the local population, and it is the primary language used in government, education, and media.

1. **Regional Accents and Dialects:**
   - While standard Portuguese is the norm, you may encounter regional accents and minor linguistic variations in different islands. These differences add to the cultural richness of the archipelago.

1. **English Language Proficiency:**
   - English is commonly spoken and understood, especially in tourist

areas, hotels, and restaurants. Many residents working in the tourist business speak English well.

1. **Basic Phrases in Portuguese:**
   - Learning a few basic phrases in Portuguese can enhance your travel experience and show respect for the local culture. Phrases such as "hello" (olá), "thank you" (Obrigado/obrigada - for males and females, respectively), and "excuse me" (com licença) are always appreciated.

1. **Language Apps and Translation Tools:**
   - Language apps and translation tools can be helpful when navigating communication barriers. Offline translation apps

can assist in understanding menus and signs when internet access is limited.

1. **Cultural Sensitivity:**
   - When speaking with natives, be patient and considerate, particularly if there are language issues. Polite gestures and a friendly demeanor go a long way in fostering positive interactions.

1. **Written Information:**
   - Most tourist-related information, such as brochures, menus, and signs at popular attractions, is available in Portuguese and English.

1. **Sign Language:**
   - Portuguese Sign Language (Língua Gestual Portuguesa - LPG) is the sign language used by

the deaf community in Portugal, including the Azores.

1. **Language Exchange:**
   - If you're interested in language exchange and cultural immersion, engaging in conversations with locals is a wonderful opportunity to learn more about the Azorean way of life.
1. **Patience and Understanding:**
   - While many locals speak English, some may be more comfortable in Portuguese. Be patient and understanding, and don't hesitate to use non-verbal communication if needed.

The Azores are a welcoming and hospitable destination, and communication is usually not a significant barrier for travelers.

1.8 Useful Phrases

Here are some basic useful phrases that you might find useful when visiting the Azores. This will make communicating with locals easier and your vacation more pleasurable:

1. **Greetings and Basic Phrases:**
    - Hello: Olá (oh-LAH)
    - Good morning: Bom dia (Bohm DEE-ah)
    - Good afternoon: Boa tarde (boh-ah TAHR-deh)
    - Good evening: Boa noite (boh-ah NOY-teh)
    - Please: Por favor (poor fah-VOHR)
    - Thank you: Obrigado (for males) / Obrigada (for females) (oh-bree-GAH-doo / oh-bree-GAH-dah)

- You're welcome: De nada (deh NAH-dah)
- Excuse me / Sorry: Desculpe (deh-SKUL-peh)
- Yes: Sim (seem)
- No: Não (now)

1. **Basic Conversational Phrases:**
   - How are you?: Como está? (Koh-moh ehs-TAH)
   - I'm fine, thank you: Estou bem, obrigado/a (esh-TOH beyhn, oh-bree-GAH-doo/dah)
   - What is your name?: Como se chama? (koh-moh seh SHAH-mah?)
   - My name is...: Chamo-me... (SHAH-moh meh...)
   - Where is...?: Onde fica...? (OHN-deh FEE-kah...?)

- How much is this?: Quanto custa isto? (KWAHN-toh KOOSH-tah EES-too?)
- I don't understand: Não entendo (now ehn-TEHN-doo)
- Can you speak English?: Fala inglês? (FAH-lah een-GLAYSH?)
- I need help: Preciso de ajuda (preh-SEE-soh deh ah-ZHOO-dah)
- Goodbye: Adeus (ah-DEH-oosh)

1. **Dining Phrases:**
   - Do you have a menu in English?: Tem um menu em inglês? (tehm oom MEH-noo ehm een-GLAYSH?)
   - Water, please: Água, por favor (AH-gwah, poor fah-VOHR)
   - I would like...: Gostaria de... (gohs-TAH-ree-ah deh...)

- The bill, please: A conta, por favor (ah KOHN-tah, poor fah-VOHR)

1. **Asking for Directions:**
   - Where is...?: Onde fica...? (OHN-deh FEE-kah...?)
   - How do I get to...?: Como chego a...? (KOH-moh SHEH-goh ah...?)
   - Is it far from here?: É longe daqui? (eh LOHN-jee dah-KEE?)

General Phrases:
- **Hello:** Olá (oh-lah)
- **Goodbye:** Adeus (ah-day-oosh)
- **Please:** Por favor (pohr fah-vohr)
- **Thank you:** Obrigado (oh-bree-gah-doh)
- **You're welcome:** De nada (day nah-dah)
- **Do you speak English?:** Fala inglês? (fah-lah ing-gleh-suh

- **I don't speak Portuguese:** Não falo português (nah-oh fa-loh poo-rtoo-gee-suh)
- **Where 's the bathroom?:** Onde é o banheiro? (ohn-day eh oh bah-nyah-roh)
- **How much does this cost?:** Quanto custa isso? (kwan-toh koo-shta ih-soh)
- **What are the finest activities in the Azores?:** Quais são as melhores coisas para fazer nas Açores? (kwahs sãw ahs mel-yeh-reh koh-zee-ngs pah-rah fah-zer nahs ah-soh-rays?)
- **Excuse me:** Com licença (kohm lee-sehn-sah)
- **I'm lost:** Estou perdido (oh-stou pehr-dee-doh)
- **Can you help me?:** Pode me ajudar? (poh-deh meh ah-ju-dahr?)
- **Do you have a map?:** Tem um mapa? (tehm oom mah-pah?)

- **Where is the nearest restaurant?:** Onde fica o restaurante mais próximo? (ohn-day fee-kah oh reh-stah-oh-rahn-teh mais proh-xee-moh?)
- **Can I have a glass of water?:** Posso ter uma água? (poh-soh tehr oh-mah oh-gwah?)
- **Do you have any vegetarian options?:** Tem opções vegetarianas? (tehm oh-psee-soh vee-zheh-tah-ree-ahs?)
- **I'm allergic to seafood:** Sou alérgico a frutos do mar (soh ah-ler-gee-ko ah froo-toos doo maah)
- **Can you recommend a good place to go hiking?:** Pode me recomendar um bom lugar para fazer uma caminhada? (poh-deh meh reh-koh-men-dahr oom bohm loo-gahr pah-rah fah-zer oh-mah kah-mee-nah-dah?)

1. **Emergency Phrases:**
    - Help!: Socorro! (soh-KOH-roh!)
    - Call the police: Chame a polícia (SHAH-meh ah poh-LEE-see-ah)
    - I need a doctor: Preciso de um médico (preh-SEE-soh deh oong MEH-dee-koo)

Learning and using these useful phrases in Portuguese will enhance your travel experience in the Azores and help you communicate with locals in a friendly and respectful manner. Don't be afraid to practice the language and immerse yourself in the local culture during your visit to this beautiful archipelago.

1.9 Safety Tips for Travelers

1. **Emergency Contacts:**
    - Familiarize yourself with local emergency numbers, such as

police (112), medical services, and your own country's closest embassy or consulate.

1. **Travel Insurance:**
   - Purchase comprehensive travel insurance that includes medical coverage, trip cancellation, and other necessary protections. Confirm that it covers activities you plan to engage in, such as hiking or water sports.

1. **Weather Awareness:**
   - The Azores' weather can be unpredictable, so stay informed about weather conditions and forecasts. Be prepared for sudden changes and carry appropriate clothing and gear for different weather scenarios.

1. **Outdoor Activities:**
- If engaging in outdoor activities like hiking, follow marked trails and safety guidelines. Inform someone of your goals and approximate time of return. Take a map, lots of water, and snacks with you. Inform a friend or family member of your plans and when you anticipate returning. If anything occurs, someone will know where to seek for you.

1. **Ocean Safety:**
   - Pay attention to ocean conditions and follow safety rules when swimming, snorkeling, or participating in water-based activities. Be cautious of strong currents, waves, and changing tides.

1. **Respect Wildlife:**
   - The Azores are home to unique flora and fauna. Respect the local wildlife, keep a safe distance, and do not disturb or feed animals.
1. **Sun Protection:**
   - The sun can be strong, so wear sunscreen with a high SPF, a wide-brimmed hat, and sunglasses to protect yourself from sunburn.
1. **Drinking Water:**
   - Tap water in the Azores is safe to drink, but some visitors may prefer bottled water. Stay hydrated, especially during outdoor activities.
1. **Road Safety:**
   - If driving, follow traffic rules and be cautious on narrow and winding roads. Be aware of local

driving customs and yield to pedestrians.

1. **Pickpocketing and Theft:**
   - Like any tourist destination, be mindful of your belongings in crowded areas. Keep your things safe and avoid showing off your affluence.

1. **Health Precautions:**
   - Check with your doctor about any required or recommended vaccinations before traveling to the Azores. Carry any required prescriptions as well as a basic first-aid kit.

1. **Local Customs and Etiquette:**
   - Familiarize yourself with local customs and traditions to show respect for the Azorean culture and way of life.

1. **Language Awareness:**
   - While English is widely spoken, learning a few basic phrases in Portuguese can be helpful and appreciated by the locals.

1. **Travel in Groups:**
   - If exploring remote areas or participating in adventure activities, consider traveling with a group or guided tour for added safety.

1. **Stay Informed:**
   - Keep abreast of travel advisories and updates from your government's official websites before and during your trip.

1. **Be aware of your surroundings:** This is especially important when you are in

unfamiliar places. Pay attention to who is around you and what is going on.

1. **Trust your instincts:** if it doesn't feel right, it probably isn't. Don't be afraid to walk away from a situation or person that makes you uncomfortable.
1. Stay in well-lit locations at all times, particularly at night. If you must walk alone at night, try to stay in well-lit areas and avoid dark alleyways or deserted streets.
1. **Carry your identification:** This includes your passport, driver's license, and any other important identification documents. If you lose your identification, it will be much more difficult to get help if something happens.
1. **Be aware of your belongings:** Don't leave your belongings unattended, especially in crowded areas. If you have

to leave your belongings, try to keep them in sight or with a trusted friend.

1. **Drink in moderation:** Alcohol may impair judgment and make you more susceptible to crime. If you do drink alcohol, do so in moderation and be aware of your surroundings.
1. **Report any suspicious activity:** If you see something that doesn't seem right, report it to the authorities. This might aid in the prevention of a crime.

By adhering to these safety tips, you can ensure a safe and enjoyable visit to the Azores, allowing you to focus on exploring the natural wonders and cultural treasures of this magnificent archipelago.

CHAPTER 2

The Islands of Azores

2.1 São Miguel

The enchanting Azores, a hidden gem in the middle of the Atlantic Ocean! Among the archipelago's nine magnificent islands, São Miguel shines like a dazzling star, a haven for travelers seeking a perfect blend of adventure, tranquility, and natural wonders. The largest island in the Azores is São Miguel, and it is a popular destination for tourists who want to experience the natural beauty of the Azores.

São Miguel is home to a variety of stunning scenery, including lush green mountains, crystal-clear lakes, and black sand beaches. Hiking, bicycling, whale viewing, and golfing are additional popular outdoor activities for visitors. In addition to its natural beauty, São

Miguel also has a rich cultural history. The island was originally settled by the Portuguese in the 15th century, and it has a unique blend of Portuguese and Azorean culture. Visitors can experience this culture by visiting the island's many historical landmarks, such as the Sete Cidades Lakes and the Furnas Volcano.

Whether you are looking for stunning scenery, outdoor adventure, or cultural experiences, São Miguel is the perfect place to visit. So what are you waiting for? Begin organizing your vacation to the Azores right now!

Here are some additional tips for visiting São Miguel:

- The best time to visit São Miguel is during the shoulder seasons (May-June and September-October). During these times, the weather is still good, but the people are lower.

- The greatest time to visit if you want to go hiking is during the summer months.
- If you are interested in whale watching, the best time to visit is from April to October.
- Be sure to try the local food! The Azores have delicious cuisine, which is influenced by Portuguese, African, and Brazilian flavors.
- Don't forget to pack for all types of weather. The Azores have a mild climate, but it can be unpredictable.

São Miguel, the crown jewel of the Azores, is a canvas where dreams and nature harmonize. From vibrant landscapes to thrilling escapades, this island paradise will capture your heart and soul. Embrace the wonder of São Miguel, where dreams come alive in the embrace of Mother Nature herself.

2.1.1 **Ponta Delgada: The Heart of the Azores**

Ponta Delgada is the capital of the Azores, a group of nine volcanic islands in the middle of the Atlantic Ocean. It is a lovely city with a rich history and culture. Ponta Delgada is known for its stunning scenery, including its black sand beaches, crystal-clear lakes, and lush green mountains. Visitors can also enjoy a variety of outdoor activities, such as hiking, biking, whale watching, and golfing.

In addition to its natural beauty, Ponta Delgada also has a rich cultural history. The city was founded in the 15th century by the Portuguese, and it has a unique blend of Portuguese and Azorean culture. Visitors can experience this culture by visiting the city's many historical landmarks, such as the São Francisco Church and the Sete Cidades Lakes.

Whether you are looking for stunning scenery, outdoor adventure, or cultural experiences,

Ponta Delgada is the perfect place to visit. So what are you waiting for?

Here are some additional tips for visiting Ponta Delgada:

- The best time to visit Ponta Delgada is during the shoulder seasons (May-June and September-October). During these times, the weather is still good, but the people are lower.
- The greatest time to visit if you want to go hiking is during the summer months.
- If you are interested in whale watching, the best time to visit is from April to October.
- Be sure to try the local food! The Azores have delicious cuisine, which is influenced by Portuguese, African, and Brazilian flavors.
- Don't forget to pack for all types of weather. The Azores have a mild climate, but it can be unpredictable.

2.1.2 **Furnas: The Jewel of the Azores**

Furnas is a small town on the island of São Miguel in the Azores. It is known for its stunning scenery, including its volcanic craters, hot springs, and lush green countryside. Visitors can also enjoy a variety of outdoor activities, such as hiking, biking, and boat tours.

In addition to its natural beauty, Furnas is also a lovely city with a rich history and culture. The town was founded in the 17th century by Portuguese settlers, and it has a unique blend of Portuguese and Azorean culture. Visitors can experience this culture by visiting the town's many historical landmarks, such as the Furnas Volcano and the Terra Nostra Botanical Garden. Whether you are looking for stunning scenery, outdoor adventure, or cultural experiences, Furnas is the perfect place to visit.

Here are some additional tips for visiting Furnas:

- The best time to visit Furnas is during the shoulder seasons (May-June and September-October).
- The greatest time to visit if you want to go hiking is during the summer months.
- If you are interested in hot springs, the best time to visit is from April to October.
- Be sure to try the local food! The Azores have delicious cuisine, which is influenced by Portuguese, African, and Brazilian flavors.

2.1.3 **Nordeste: The Wild Side of the Azores**

Nordeste is a municipality on the island of São Miguel in the Azores. It is known for its stunning scenery, including its rugged coastline, lush green mountains, and beautiful waterfalls.

Hiking, riding, and swimming are among the outdoor activities available to visitors.

In addition to its natural beauty, Nordeste is also a lovely city with a rich history and culture. The municipality was founded in the 16th century by Portuguese settlers, and it has a unique blend of Portuguese and Azorean culture. Visitors can experience this culture by visiting the municipality's many historical landmarks, such as the Sete Cidades Lakes and the Miradouro da Ponta do Arnel.

Whether you are looking for stunning scenery, outdoor adventure, or cultural experiences, Nordeste is the perfect place to visit.

Here are some additional tips for visiting Nordeste:

- The best time to visit Nordeste is during the shoulder seasons (May-June and September-October).

- If you are interested in swimming, the best time to visit is from May to September.
- Be sure to try the local food! The Azores have delicious cuisine, which is influenced by Portuguese, African, and Brazilian flavors.

2.2 **Terceira: The Island of History and Adventure**

Terceira is the third-largest island in the Azores where Terceira stands as a timeless masterpiece waiting to be discovered. With its rich history, vibrant culture, and stunning landscapes, Terceira is an island that promises unforgettable experiences for every traveler.

1. Terceira: Where Past Meets Present: Step onto the shores of Terceira and step back in time as cobbled streets, historic towns, and centuries-old architecture weaves a tapestry of the island's captivating past.

2. Angra do Heroísmo: A World Heritage Gem: Explore Angra do Heroísmo, a UNESCO World Heritage Site that is enchanting with its colonial charm, colorful buildings, and a historic center that whispers tales of exploration.

3. Monte Brasil: Natural Wonder on the Horizon: Conquer the majestic Monte Brasil, a dormant volcano that rises dramatically from the sea, offering panoramic vistas and a glimpse into Terceira's geological marvels.

4. Algar do Carvão: Journey into Earth's Heart: Descend into the heart of Terceira at Algar do Carvão, a volcanic chimney-turned-cavern that reveals a subterranean world adorned with shimmering stalactites.

5. Festivals that Ignite the Soul: Join the locals in vibrant festivals, like Sanjoaninas, where the island comes alive with music, dance, and traditions that celebrate Terceira's spirit.

6. The Breathtaking Coastal Beauty: Stroll along Terceira's captivating coastline, where rocky shores, hidden coves, and dramatic cliffs stand as a testament to the island's unspoiled natural beauty.

7. Graciosa and Serene: Embark on a short ferry ride to Graciosa, Terceira's serene sister island, known for its tranquil landscapes, rolling hills, and unique vineyards.

8. Water Adventures Await: Dive into a world of aquatic wonder as Terceira offers a playground for water enthusiasts, from diving in underwater caves to exploring azure lagoons.

9. Quintas and Culinary Delights: Savor the flavors of Terceira's rich cuisine, from traditional alcatra stews to fresh seafood, while enjoying the hospitality of Quintas – charming countryside estates.

10. Sunsets Over Praia da Vitória: Watch the sun set over Praia da Vitória's golden shores, painting the sky with hues of oranges and purples, a magical end to your day in Terceira.

Terceira, a fusion of history and nature, culture and adventure, stands as a testament to the Azores' allure. Explore its cobblestone streets, embrace its traditions, and immerse yourself in its breathtaking landscapes. Terceira welcomes you to uncover the timeless treasures that have shaped its soul.

2.2.1 **Angra do Heroísmo: The Jewel of the Azores**

Welcome to Angra do Heroísmo, the heart, and soul of Terceira Island in the Azores archipelago. With its rich history, charming streets, and awe-inspiring vistas, this UNESCO World Heritage city is a destination that beckons travelers to uncover its timeless beauty and captivating tales.

1. Angra's Historic Tapestry: Step into Angra do Heroísmo and step back in time.

Cobblestone streets, centuries-old architecture, and colorful facades come together to create a living tapestry of history.

2. Praça Velha: The Heart of Angra: Discover Praça Velha, the heart of the city, where vibrant cafes, historic buildings, and a sense of community transport you to a bygone era.

3. Sé Catedral: Echoes of the Past: Visit Sé Catedral, the city's majestic cathedral that stands as a testament to Angra's enduring faith and architectural grandeur.

4. Monte Brasil: Nature's Fortress of Legends: Climb Monte Brasil, an ancient volcanic cone turned fortress, where panoramic views reveal the city's charming streets, lush landscapes, and the vast Atlantic horizon.

5. Praia da Vitória: A Coastal Escape: Venture to Praia da Vitória, a neighboring town known for its golden sands, inviting waters, and a sense of tranquility that rejuvenates the soul.

6. Algar do Carvão: A Glimpse Below: Descend into Algar do Carvão, a mystical volcanic chimney that leads to an underground world adorned with stunning formations, a true wonder of nature.

7. Festas Sanjoaninas: Dance of Tradition: Immerse yourself in the vibrant Festas Sanjoaninas, an annual celebration where locals and visitors alike come together to dance, feast, and revel in Terceira's spirit.

8. Whispers of the Past: Angra's Museums: Explore Angra's museums, from the Museu de Angra do Heroísmo to the Núcleo de História Militar, each offering a glimpse into the island's storied past.

9. Culinary Delights: A Gastronomic Journey: Savor Angra's culinary delights, from traditional cozido stews to fresh seafood, as you dine amidst the city's enchanting atmosphere.

10. Sunset Magic at Alto da Memória: Witness the sun's glorious descent from Alto da

Memória, where the sky transforms into a canvas of colors, casting a binding spell over Angra.

Angra do Heroísmo is more than a city; it's a journey through time, a celebration of culture, and a gateway to Terceira's soul. Let its historic streets, panoramic views, and warm community spirit embrace you as you write your tale within its timeless embrace.

2.2.2 Praia da Vitória: The Perfect Place to Relax, Where Tranquility Meets Coastal Beauty

Praia da Vitória is a picturesque gem nestled on the shores of Terceira Island in the Azores. With its golden beaches, serene landscapes, and welcoming atmosphere, this charming town invites you to experience a perfect blend of relaxation and coastal beauty.

1. Praia da Vitória: Seaside Serenity: Step into the tranquility of Praia da Vitória, where the rhythms of the ocean harmonize with the island's laid-back charm, offering a haven for seekers of peace.

2. Golden Sands and Azure Waters: Indulge in the allure of Praia da Vitória's golden sands and crystal-clear waters, where the beach becomes your sanctuary for relaxation and sun-kissed memories.

3. Marina Delight: A Sailor's Haven: Explore the town's marina, a haven for sailors and lovers of the sea, where yachts and boats sway gently amidst a backdrop of endless blue.

4. Histórias Infinitas Park: Nature's Playground: Discover Histórias Infinitas Park, a vibrant green space that beckons with walking paths, picnic spots, and a place where nature's beauty unfolds.

5. Monte Brasil's Embrace: Panoramic Perspectives: Ascend Monte Brasil to witness panoramic views that embrace the town, revealing a patchwork of rooftops, serene waters, and the breathtaking expanse of the Atlantic.

6. Praça Francisco Ornelas da Câmara: The Heartbeat of Town: Immerse yourself in local life at Praça Francisco Ornelas da Câmara, a lively square where cafes, boutiques, and culture converge.

7. Lighthouse of Ponta da Serreta: A Guiding Light: Journey to the Lighthouse of Ponta da Serreta, where the captivating coastline and endless horizon blend into a poetic sunset, a sight to behold.

8. Terceira's Taste: Gastronomic Delights: Savor the island's flavors at Praia da Vitória's restaurants, where fresh seafood and local specialties make every meal a culinary journey.

9. Cultural Gems: Uncover History's Veil: Explore the town's historical sites, like the Monumento ao Emigrante, which pays homage to those who embarked on journeys of hope and exploration.

10. Sunset Serenade at Praia Grande: Nature's Farewell: Bask in the magic of a Praia Grande sunset, where the sky ignites with hues of gold and crimson, bidding a serene farewell to another day in paradise.

Praia da Vitória is a coastal haven where time slows down, allowing you to reconnect with nature and yourself. Let its peaceful beaches, charming streets, and warm hospitality create memories that linger long after you leave, reminding you of the simple beauty found in this seaside paradise.

2.3 Faial: The Blue Island Where Adventure and Serenity Converge

Faial is an island where adventure and serenity intertwine amidst captivating landscapes. Nestled within the Azores archipelago, Faial is the westernmost of the nine Azores islands, and it is the fourth largest. The island is volcanic in origin, and it is home to several craters and calderas. The island is also home to a variety of plant life, including hydrangeas, which bloom in shades of blue, pink, and purple. Faial beckons travelers to explore its natural wonders, vibrant culture, and breathtaking vistas.

1. Faial's Enchanting Aura: Step onto the shores of Faial and feel the island's enchanting aura embrace you, inviting you to embark on an unforgettable journey.

2. Caldeira: Nature's Bowl of Wonders: Discover Caldeira, a majestic volcanic crater that unveils panoramic views of lush landscapes, forming a natural amphitheater that stirs the soul.

3. Horta: A Harbor of Dreams: Explore Horta, the island's charming harbor town adorned with colorful marinas, historic buildings, and an artistic spirit that paints every corner.

4. Marina Murals: An Artistic Oasis: Marvel at Horta's marina murals, a canvas where sailors and artists converge, leaving their mark on the town's vibrant culture.

5. Capelinhos: Volcanic Marvel Unveiled: Unearth the captivating story of Capelinhos, a volcanic eruption that birthed a new landscape, creating an otherworldly setting that captivates the imagination.

6. Porto Pim: Tranquility by the Sea: Relax at Porto Pim, a serene beach where azure waters meet golden sands, offering a tranquil haven for unwinding and water adventures.

7. Scenic Drives and Overlooks: Embark on scenic drives that lead to breathtaking viewpoints, like the Espalamaca Viewpoint, where the island's beauty stretches out before you.

8. Peter Café Sport: A Maritime Legend: Visit the iconic Peter Café Sport, a maritime institution that weaves tales of seafaring adventures, offering a warm welcome and a taste of local life.

9. Whales and Dolphins: Ocean Encounters: Embark on a whale-watching adventure to encounter majestic marine life, a testament to Faial's deep connection with the ocean.

10. Sunset Magic at Ponta do Castelo: Nature's Grand Finale: Witness the sun's grand finale at Ponta do Castelo, where fiery sunsets cast a spell over the island, painting the sky in hues of gold and crimson.

Faial is a symphony of experiences, where nature's wonders and human stories blend harmoniously. From volcanic marvels to tranquil beaches, from artistic havens to maritime legends, this island offers a tapestry of adventures waiting to be woven into your journey. Faial welcomes you to embrace its allure and create memories that will forever echo in your heart.

2.3.1 Horta: Where Colors and Stories Collide Horta

Horta is a port town on the island of Faial in the Azores archipelago. It is known for its colorful houses, its vibrant nightlife, and its friendliest town in the Azores.

Horta is the largest town on Faial, and it is a popular destination for tourists. The town is located on a beautiful bay, and it is surrounded by hills. The houses in Horta are painted in bright colors, which gives the town a cheerful atmosphere. A town that dances between the realms of history and artistry on the enchanting island of Faial. Horta beckons you to explore its kaleidoscope of colors, maritime heritage, and captivating tales.

1. Horta's Charismatic Canvas: Welcome to Horta, where every street is a brushstroke and every corner a masterpiece, weaving a charismatic canvas that celebrates life, culture, and the sea.

2. Marina Murals: Harbor of Expression: Marvel at Horta's marina murals, where sailors and artists leave their mark, transforming the town's harbor into an ever-evolving gallery of creativity.

3. Icons of Adventure: Peter Café Sport: Embrace the maritime spirit at Peter Café Sport, an icon where sailors' stories blend with the aroma of coffee and camaraderie, enriching the town's heritage.

4. Port of Call: Maritime Melodies: Discover Horta's role as a historic port of call for sailors across the globe, where tales of journeys echo in every seafaring breeze.

5. Porto Pim: Serenity by the Shore: Escape to Porto Pim, a tranquil beach where azure waters meet golden sands, inviting you to unwind, bask in the sun, and embark on aquatic adventures.

6. Espalamaca Viewpoint: Panoramic Poetry: Ascend to the Espalamaca Viewpoint, where sweeping vistas of Horta's picturesque harbor and the vast Atlantic Ocean become a canvas of panoramic poetry.

7. Historical Charm: Monte da Guia: Explore the historic charm of Monte da Guia, a headland that reveals a charming lighthouse, botanical gardens, and breathtaking coastal vistas.

8. Whales and Dolphins: Ocean's Melody: Embark on an oceanic symphony with whale-watching adventures that unveil the majestic melodies of marine life, connecting you to the heart of Horta's waters.

9. Culinary Delights: Flavorful Notes: Savor Horta's culinary delights, where seafood dishes and local flavors harmonize with the island's essence, creating a taste of authentic Azorean life.

10. Sunset Magic at Praia do Almoxarife: Nature's Grand Finale: Witness the sun's grand finale at Praia do Almoxarife, where the sky ignites with hues of wonder, bidding a serene farewell to another day in paradise.

Horta is a vibrant symphony of colors, stories, and experiences that linger in your heart. From artistic marinas to historic icons, from panoramic vistas to oceanic melodies, this town welcomes you to dive into its tapestry of life, creating memories that will forever illuminate your journey.

2.4 **Pico: Where Nature and Adventure Reach New Heights**

Welcome to Pico, the second-largest island in the Azores archipelago, it is known for its stunning volcanic landscapes. The island is home to the highest mountain in Portugal, Pico Mountain, which is an active volcano.

Pico is also home to a variety of other volcanic features, including craters, calderas, and lava fields. Visitors can enjoy hiking, biking, and horseback riding on the island to explore these natural wonders with its towering peak and captivating charm, Pico promises an unforgettable journey of discovery.

1. Pico's Peaks and Valleys: Step into the embrace of Pico's dramatic landscapes, where lush valleys and towering peaks create a stunning contrast that defines the island's character.

2. Montanha do Pico: Summit of Dreams: Conquer Montanha do Pico, the highest peak in Portugal, and stand atop a volcano that offers panoramic views of a world that stretches from sky to sea.

3. Whales and Dolphins: Oceanic Symphony: Embark on a marine adventure to witness the majestic symphony of whales and dolphins, a testament to Pico's deep connection with the Atlantic.

4. Vineyards and Wines: Tastes of Terroir: Savor Pico's renowned wines are nurtured in vineyards that thrive amidst black lava fields, reflecting the island's unique terroir and history.

5. Lajes do Pico: Maritime Heritage Unveiled: Explore Lajes do Pico, a historic whaling town that tells tales of seafaring traditions and maritime legacies etched into the very fabric of the island.

6. Pico's Caves: Underground Wonders: Delve into Pico's underground world of caves and lava tubes, where nature's artistry unfolds in dark chambers and breathtaking formations.

7. São Roque do Pico: Gateway to Adventure: Discover São Roque do Pico, a charming town that serves as a gateway to Pico's adventures, from hiking to diving to exploring lunar-like landscapes.

8. Pico's Culture: Whispers of the Past: Immerse yourself in Pico's culture through its museums, festivals, and traditions, capturing the island's heritage and the echoes of its people.

9. São Jorge Island: A Neighboring Gem: Embark on an island-hopping escapade to São Jorge, Pico's neighboring gem, known for its rugged beauty, charming villages, and stunning cliffs.

10. Sunset Spectacle at Ponta da Ilha: Nature's Grand Finale: Witness the sun's breathtaking descent from Ponta da Ilha, where the horizon transforms into a canvas of colors, bidding a serene farewell to the day.

Pico is a symphony of adventure, nature, and heritage, where every corner reveals a new facet of its captivating beauty. From mountain peaks to ocean depths, from historic towns to underground wonders, Pico invites you to explore its vast landscapes and create memories that will forever elevate your spirit.

2.4.1 Madalena: The Heart of Pico Where Beauty and Adventure Unite

Madalena is the largest town on the island of Pico in the Azores archipelago. It is known for its charming streets, its beautiful scenery, and its delicious food.

Madalena is located on the western coast of Pico, and it is surrounded by mountains and vineyards. The town is home to a variety of shops, restaurants, and bars. Visitors can enjoy strolling through the streets of Madalena, sampling the local food, and taking in the views of the surrounding countryside.

1. Madalena's Coastal Elegance: Welcome to Madalena, where the town's elegance merges with the stunning beauty of the surrounding coastline, creating a captivating haven for travelers.

2. Vineyards and Vistas: Wine Trails of Wonder: Wander through Pico's iconic vineyards, a UNESCO World Heritage site, and savor the flavors of wines cultivated in unique black lava soil.

3. Montanha do Pico: Towering Dreams: Gaze in awe at Montanha do Pico, the towering peak that stands as both a natural wonder and a challenge for adventurers seeking to conquer its summit.

4. Whales and Dolphins: Oceanic Encounters: Embark on a marine journey to encounter the graceful giants of the ocean, whales and dolphins, that call the waters near Madalena their home.

5. Museu do Vinho: Tales of Terroir: Explore Museu do Vinho, a museum dedicated to the island's wine culture, where tales of traditions and history are told through exhibits and artifacts.

6. Praia do Canto: Tranquility by the Shore: Relax at Praia do Canto, a serene beach where the gentle lapping of waves invites you to unwind and bask in the sun's warm embrace.

7. Pico Island: Island-Hopping Adventure: Venture beyond Madalena to explore Pico Island's diverse landscapes, from volcanic peaks to hidden coves, creating a tapestry of adventures.

8. Madalena's Markets: Local Flavors and Crafts: Stroll through Madalena's markets, where the aroma of fresh produce mingles with local crafts, offering a taste of the town's vibrant culture.

9. São Jorge Island: A Neighboring Gem: Embark on an island-hopping escapade to São Jorge, Pico's neighboring gem, known for its scenic beauty, lush landscapes, and vibrant communities.

10. Sunset Symphony at Cabeço da Queimada: Nature's Grand Finale: Witness the sun's serene descent from Cabeço da Queimada, where the horizon becomes a canvas of colors, bidding a poetic farewell to the day.

Madalena is a harmonious blend of beauty and adventure, where nature's wonders and human stories intertwine. From vineyards to peaks, from marine encounters to cultural treasures, this town invites you to immerse yourself in its charm, creating memories that will forever resonate in your heart.

2.5 São Jorge: The Island of Contrasts, Symphony of Nature and Serenity

São Jorge is an island in the Azores archipelago, located in the middle of the Atlantic Ocean. It is known for its stunning scenery, its varied landscapes, and its friendly people.

São Jorge is the longest of the nine Azores islands, and it is shaped like a whale. The island is home to a variety of landscapes, including lush green valleys, rugged mountains, and black sand beaches. Visitors can enjoy hiking, biking, and swimming in the island's many natural beauty spots.

1. São Jorge's Natural Sonata: Step into São Jorge's enchanting world, where nature's symphony plays out in rolling hills, dramatic cliffs, and azure waters that stretch to the horizon.

2. Fajãs: Nature's Hidden Gems: Discover the unique Fajãs, lush flatlands nestled between cliffs and the sea, where life thrives in harmony with the island's diverse landscapes.

3. Calheta: A Coastal Oasis: Explore Calheta, a picturesque coastal town where white houses and colorful boats create a charming scene against the backdrop of the deep blue ocean.

4. Queijo São Jorge: A Taste of Tradition: Savor the island 's famed Queijo São Jorge, a cheese crafted with generations of expertise, embodying São Jorge' s culinary heritage.

5. Ponta dos Rosais: Panoramic Beauty: Witness the panoramic beauty of Ponta dos

Rosais, where cliffs meet the Atlantic, offering sweeping views that capture the essence of São Jorge.

6. São Jorge's Festivals: Celebrations of Life: Immerse yourself in São Jorge's vibrant festivals, where music, dance, and traditions come together to celebrate the island's rich cultural heritage.

7. Fajã da Caldeira de Santo Cristo: Paradise Rediscovered: Visit Fajã da Caldeira de Santo Cristo, a remote paradise where natural pools, lush landscapes, and a sense of seclusion create a haven for seekers of tranquility.

8. Whale-Watching Adventures: Oceanic Encounters: Embark on whale-watching adventures to witness majestic marine life, a reminder of São Jorge's deep connection to the ocean.

9. São Jorge's Craftsmanship: Treasures of Artistry: Discover São Jorge's rich craftsmanship through its intricate pottery, woven crafts, and artistic expressions that tell tales of the island's soul.

10. Sunset Splendor at Ponta dos Rosais: Nature's Grand Finale: Behold the sun's breathtaking descent from Ponta dos Rosais, where the horizon transforms into a canvas of colors, bidding a serene farewell to the day.

São Jorge is a symphony of natural beauty and cultural treasures, where every corner reveals a piece of its serene allure. From Fajãs to festivals, from cliffs to culinary delights, the island invites you to explore, embrace, and create memories that will forever resonate in your heart.

2.5.1 **Velas: The Hidden Gem of São Jorge Where Timeless Beauty Meets Tranquility**

Velas is a municipality on the island of São Jorge in the Azores archipelago. It is known for its stunning scenery, its friendly people, and its laid-back atmosphere.

Velas is located on the northern coast of São Jorge, and it is surrounded by mountains and valleys. The municipality is home to a variety of beaches, hiking trails, and vineyards. Visitors can enjoy swimming, sunbathing, hiking, and wine tasting in Velas. Velas invites you to discover its timeless beauty, immerse yourself in its culture, and find solace in its peaceful corners.

1. Velas: A Gateway to Serenity: Welcome to Velas, where the pace of life slows down, and the town's elegance blends seamlessly with the stunning natural beauty that surrounds it.

2. Praça da República: The Heart of Velas: Explore Praça da República, the town's central square where history and modern life converge amidst charming architecture and vibrant cafes.

3. Fajãs: Nature's Hidden Treasures: Discover the unique Fajãs, lush coastal plains nestled between cliffs and the sea, each a microcosm of life thriving in harmony with nature.

4. Iglesia Matriz de São Jorge: Architectural Elegance: Visit the Iglesia Matriz de São Jorge, an architectural masterpiece that stands as a testament to the island's rich heritage and faith.

5. Calheta Harbor: Tranquility by the Sea: Embrace the tranquility of Calheta Harbor, where colorful boats gently sway in the calm waters, inviting you to relax and unwind.

6. Fajã de Santo Cristo: Nature's Sanctuary: Venture to Fajã de Santo Cristo, a secluded paradise where natural pools, rolling hills, and a sense of isolation create a haven for seekers of peace.

7. Cultural Flavors: Gastronomic Delights: Savor Velas' culinary delights, from fresh seafood to local specialties, as you dine amidst the town's charming atmosphere.

8. Whale-Watching Wonders: Oceanic Encounters: Embark on whale-watching adventures to witness the majestic marine life that graces Velas' shores, connecting you to the heart of the ocean.

9. Craftsmanship and Artistry: Treasures of Culture: Explore Velas' craftsmanship, from intricate ceramics to handwoven textiles, each piece telling a story of the island's culture and heritage.

10. Sunset Splendor at Ponta dos Rosais: Nature's Grand Finale: Witness the sun's breathtaking descent from Ponta dos Rosais, where the sky becomes a canvas of colors, bidding a serene farewell to the day.

Velas is a harmonious blend of beauty and tranquility, where nature's wonders and human stories unite. From charming streets to hidden fajãs, from historic architecture to culinary delights, Velas welcomes you to explore, embrace, and create memories that will forever echo in your heart.

2.6 **Graciosa: The Gentle Island Where Serenity and Charm Blossom**

Graciosa is an island in the Azores archipelago, located in the middle of the Atlantic Ocean. It is known for its gentle terrain, its friendly people, and it's delicious food.

Graciosa is the smallest of the central group of Azores islands, and it is shaped like a heart. The island is home to a variety of landscapes, including rolling hills, vineyards, and black-sand beaches. Visitors can enjoy hiking, biking, swimming, and whale watching in Graciosa.

1. Graciosa's Tranquil Allure: Step onto the shores of Graciosa and feel the island's tranquil allure embrace you, offering a respite from the bustle of everyday life.

2. Santa Cruz da Graciosa: A Town Frozen in Time: Explore Santa Cruz da Graciosa, a town that feels like a charming time capsule, where cobblestone streets and traditional houses whisper tales of the past.

3. Furna do Enxofre: A Subterranean Wonderland: Descend into the depths of Furna do Enxofre, a volcanic cave adorned with stunning formations, offering an otherworldly experience.

4. Praia: The Gem of Calmness: Relax at Praia, a serene beach with inviting waters and a sense of serenity that washes over you, inviting you to unwind.

5. Graciosa's Windmills: Guardians of Tradition: Discover Graciosa's iconic windmills, which stand as guardians of tradition, embodying the island's agricultural heritage.

6. Furna do Abel: Cavern of Wonders: Marvel at Furna do Abel, a cave that mesmerizes with its intricate stalactites and stalagmites, creating a natural spectacle.

7. Wine Culture and Vineyards: Taste of Terroir: Savor the taste of Graciosas wines, cultivated in unique vineyards that thrive amidst the island's lush landscapes.

8. Marine Encounters: Whales and Dolphins Await: Embark on marine adventures to encounter whales and dolphins, a reminder of Graciosas deep connection to the ocean.

9. Coastal Trails and Scenic Views: Nature's Pathways: Explore Graciosas coastal trails that lead to stunning viewpoints, offering panoramic vistas of the island's beauty.

10. Sunset Serenade at Ponta da Barca: Nature's Grand Finale: Witness the sun's serene descent from Ponta da Barca, where the horizon becomes a canvas of colors, bidding a poetic farewell to the day.

Graciosa is a haven of serenity and charm, where every moment is an invitation to embrace the island's natural beauty and rich heritage. From historic towns to hidden caves, from lush landscapes to tranquil beaches, Graciosa welcomes you to explore, immerse, and create memories that will forever bloom in your heart.

2.6.1 Santa Cruz da Graciosa: The White Island with Timeless Charms and Tranquil Delights

Santa Cruz da Graciosa is the capital of the island of Graciosa in the Azores archipelago. It is known for its whitewashed houses, its charming streets, and its stunning views.

Santa Cruz da Graciosa is located on the western coast of Graciosa, and it is surrounded by vineyards and rolling hills. The town is home to a variety of shops, restaurants, and bars. Visitors can enjoy strolling through the streets of Santa Cruz da Graciosa, sampling the local food, and taking in the views of the surrounding countryside.

1. Santa Cruz da Graciosa: A Quaint Haven: Welcome to Santa Cruz da Graciosa, where cobblestone streets, traditional architecture, and a sense of calmness create a haven for seekers of peace.

2. Praça Fontes Pereira de Melo: Heartbeat of Town: Explore Praça Fontes Pereira de Melo, the vibrant heart of the town, where locals gather, and history unfolds amidst charming cafes and historic buildings.

3. Igreja Matriz de Santa Cruz: Architectural Elegance: Visit Igreja Matriz de Santa Cruz, a stunning church that stands as a testament to the town's deep-rooted faith and architectural beauty.

4. Furna do Enxofre: Subterranean Marvel: Descend into Furna do Enxofre, a subterranean marvel adorned with fascinating formations, inviting you to discover the island's geological wonders.

5. Lagoa do Negro: Tranquil Oasis: Find tranquility at Lagoa do Negro, a serene lake surrounded by lush vegetation, creating a peaceful oasis for reflection and relaxation.

6. Windmills of Graciosa: Guardians of Tradition: Discover the iconic windmills of Graciosa, symbols of the island's agricultural heritage, where time seems to stand still.

7. Coastal Trails and Vistas: Nature's Pathways: Embark on coastal trails that lead to breathtaking viewpoints, where panoramic vistas of the ocean and landscapes unfold before you.

8. Festa de São João: Festive Traditions: Immerse yourself in Festa de São João, a vibrant festival where music, dancing, and local traditions celebrate the island's cultural heritage.

9. Whale-Watching Adventures: Oceanic Encounters: Venture into the ocean for unforgettable whale-watching adventures, connecting you to the marine life that graces Santa Cruz da Graciosa's shores.

10. Sunset Harmony at Ponta da Barca: Nature's Grand Finale: Witness the sun's graceful descent from Ponta da Barca, where the horizon transforms into a canvas of colors, bidding a serene farewell to the day.

Santa Cruz da Graciosa is a treasure trove of timeless charm and tranquil beauty, where every corner exudes a sense of serenity. From historic squares to hidden caves, from architectural elegance to coastal vistas, the town welcomes you to explore, immerse, and create memories that will forever echo in your heart.

2.7 **Flores: The Island of Waterfalls Where Nature's Palette Unfolds**

Flores is an Azores archipelago island in the center of the Atlantic Ocean. It is known for its stunning scenery, its abundant waterfalls, and its friendly people.

Flores is the westernmost island of the Azores, and it is shaped like a flower. The island is home to a variety of landscapes, including lush green valleys, rugged mountains, and black sand beaches. Visitors can enjoy hiking, biking, swimming, and whale watching in Flores.

1. Flores' Living Canvas: Step onto the canvas of Flores, where rolling hills, pristine lakes, and vibrant flowers create a living masterpiece that captures the soul.

2. Lagoa das Sete Cidades: The Lake of Seven Colors: Discover Lagoa das Sete Cidades, a captivating lake with hues that shift like a painter's palette, creating a surreal and breathtaking spectacle.

3. Ponta Delgada: Coastal Beauty Unveiled: Explore Ponta Delgada, a charming coastal town where colorful houses and a picturesque harbor invite you to discover a world of seaside tranquility.

4. Rocha dos Bordões: Nature's Artistry Unveiled: Marvel at Rocha dos Bordões, towering basalt columns that rise like ancient monoliths, revealing nature's sculptural artistry.

5. Fajã Grande: A Secluded Paradise: Escape to Fajã Grande, a hidden paradise nestled between cliffs and the sea, where waterfalls cascade into natural pools and serenity reigns.

6. Miradouros: Vistas of Wonder: Embark on a journey of discovery through Flores' miradouros, where panoramic vistas showcase the island's breathtaking beauty from every angle.

7. Flores' Waterfalls: Cascading Beauty: Delight in Flores' waterfalls, where cascades plunge into emerald pools, creating a symphony of nature's beauty that resonates in the heart.

8. Ponta da Fajã: Oceanic Symphony: Witness the ocean's symphony at Ponta da Fajã, where waves crash against cliffs in a mesmerizing dance that reflects the island's rugged charm.

9. Festivals and Traditions: Cultural Celebrations: Immerse yourself in Flores' festivals, where music, dance, and traditions come alive, celebrating the island's rich cultural heritage.

10. Sunset Splendor at Miradouro da Rocha Alta: Nature's Grand Finale: Behold the sun's radiant descent from Miradouro da Rocha Alta, where the sky transforms into a canvas of colors, bidding a serene farewell to the day.

Flores is a testament to the wonders of nature's brush, where every vista is a masterpiece waiting to be explored. From lakes to waterfalls, from coastal towns to hidden paradises, the island invites you to uncover its secrets, immerse in its beauty, and create memories that will forever bloom in your heart.

2.7.1 Santa Cruz das Flores: The Jewel of Flores Where Tranquility Meets Coastal Charm

Step into the serene embrace of Santa Cruz das Flores, the capital of the island of Flores with a coastal gem on the island of Flores within the Azores archipelago. Santa Cruz das Flores is located on the western coast of Flores, and it is surrounded by lush green hills and valleys with its picturesque landscapes, charming streets, and inviting atmosphere, Santa Cruz das Flores invites you to discover its timeless beauty, embrace its rich history, and find solace in its tranquil surroundings.

1. Santa Cruz das Flores: Coastal Elegance: Welcome to Santa Cruz das Flores, where coastal elegance and natural beauty unite, creating a haven of serenity and charm.

2. Praça Almirante D'Andrade: Heartbeat of Town: Explore Praça Almirante D'Andrade, the town's central square where history and modern life converge, inviting you to relax and soak in the ambiance.

3. Igreja de Nossa Senhora da Conceição: Architectural Grace: Visita à Igreja de Nossa Senhora da Conceição, a beautiful church that stands as a testament to Santa Cruz das Flores' deep-rooted faith and architectural splendor.

4. Ponta do Albarnaz: Coastal Beauty Unveiled: Discover Ponta do Albarnaz, where rugged cliffs meet the endless expanse of the Atlantic Ocean, offering stunning vistas that captivate the soul.

5. Lagoa do Pomar: Tranquil Oasis: Escape to Lagoa do Pomar, a serene lake surrounded by lush vegetation, creating a peaceful oasis for reflection and relaxation.

6. Miradouros: Vistas of Wonder: Embark on a journey of discovery through Santa Cruz das Flores' miradouros, where panoramic views showcase the island's natural beauty in all its glory.

7. Fajãs: Hidden Coastal Treasures: Explore the unique Fajãs, coastal flatlands that nestle between cliffs and the sea, each a treasure trove of life and beauty shaped by nature.

8. Festas e Traditions: Cultural Celebrations: Immerse yourself in Santa Cruz das Flores' festivals, where music, dance, and traditions come together to celebrate the island's vibrant culture.

9. Marine Encounters: Whales and Dolphins Await: Embark on marine adventures to encounter whales and dolphins, connecting you to the marine life that graces Santa Cruz das Flores' shores.

10. Sunset Harmony at Ponta da Rocha: Nature's Grand Finale: Witness the sun's graceful descent from Ponta da Rocha, where the horizon transforms into a canvas of colors, bidding a serene farewell to the day.

Santa Cruz das Flores is a haven of coastal charm and tranquility, where every corner invites you to unwind and embrace the beauty of the natural world. From historic squares to breathtaking viewpoints, from architectural elegance to cultural celebrations, the town welcomes you to explore, immerse, and create memories that will forever resonate in your heart.

2.8 **Corvo: The Smallest Island in the Azores with a Jewel of Solitude and Splendor**

Welcome to Corvo, the smallest island in the Azores archipelago, located in the middle of the Atlantic Ocean. Corvo is only 17 kilometers long and 7 kilometers wide, making it the smallest of the nine Azores islands. A remote jewel that beckons you with its untouched beauty, tranquil landscapes, and unique charm. With its rugged allure, abundant nature, and quiet serenity, Corvo invites you to explore its untouched corners, immerse yourself in its natural wonders, and discover the hidden treasures of this secluded island.

1. Corvo's Enchanted Solitude: Step onto the shores of Corvo, where untouched landscapes and the soothing sounds of nature envelop you in an enchanting cocoon of solitude.

2. Caldeirão: A Crater of Wonder: Discover Caldeirão, the awe-inspiring volcanic crater that cradles a serene lake, a testament to the island's geological marvels.

3. Vila do Corvo: A Hamlet of Tranquility: Explore Vila do Corvo, a charming hamlet that exudes a sense of timelessness, inviting you to discover the island's unhurried pace.

4. Miradouros: Vistas of Awe: Embark on a journey through Corvo's miradouros, where panoramic vistas offer breathtaking views that capture the island's raw beauty.

5. Caldeira do Cabeço do Gordo: Summit of Wonders: Ascend Caldeira do Cabeço do Gordo, a volcanic peak that rewards you with sweeping views, a canvas where nature's palette unfolds.

6. Natural Pools: Oceanic Oases: Delight in Corvo's natural pools, where crystal-clear waters nestled amidst dramatic cliffs offer a refreshing haven for relaxation.

7. Marine Encounters: Whales and Dolphins Await: Embark on marine adventures to encounter whales and dolphins, a reminder of Corvo's deep connection to the Atlantic's marine life.

8. Festivals and Traditions: Cultural Celebrations: Immerse yourself in Corvo's festivals, where music, dance, and traditions showcase the island's vibrant cultural heritage.

9. Sunset Splendor at Miradouro do Cabeço: Nature's Grand Finale: Witness the sun's serene descent from Miradouro do Cabeço, where the horizon transforms into a canvas of colors, bidding a tranquil farewell to the day.

10. Corvo's Untamed Beauty: An Everlasting Memory: Corvo's untamed beauty creates an everlasting memory, where each moment is an invitation to discover nature's untouched wonders and create memories that linger in your heart.

Corvo is a jewel of solitude and splendor, where the pace of life matches the rhythm of nature. From volcanic wonders to panoramic views, from tranquil pools to cultural celebrations, the island welcomes you to explore, immerse, and create a lasting connection with its untouched treasures.

2.8.1 **Vila do Corvo: The Tiny Jewel of the Azores Where Time Stands Still and Nature Thrives**

Welcome to Vila do Corvo the capital of the island of Corvo in the Azores archipelago.It is well-known for its beautiful scenery, friendly people, and laid-back attitude.

Vila do Corvo is the smallest capital in the Azores, with a population of just over 400 people. The town is located on the southern coast of the island, and it is surrounded by lush green hills and a crater lake.

1. Vila do Corvo: A Glimpse of Tranquility: Enter Vila do Corvo, a picturesque village where the unhurried pace of life and the island's natural beauty combine to create a sense of tranquil serenity.

2. Praça do Campo: Heart of the Village: Discover Praça do Campo, the heart of the village, where historic buildings and local cafes converge, inviting you to unwind and soak in the ambiance.

3. Igreja Nossa Senhora dos Milagres: Architectural Gem: Visita à Igreja Nossa Senhora dos Milagres, a charming church that stands as a testament to Vila do Corvo 's rich history and architectural elegance.

4. Caldeirão: Cradle of Natural Beauty: Discover Caldeirão, a volcanic crater that cradles lush vegetation and serene waters, inviting you to connect with the island's untouched splendor.

5. Baía do Corvo: Coastal Charm: Delight in the beauty of Baía do Corvo, where the rugged coastline meets the azure waters of the Atlantic Ocean, creating a tranquil coastal haven.

6. Marine Marvels: Oceanic Encounters: Embark on marine adventures to encounter the marine life that thrives in Corvo's waters, a reminder of the island's deep connection to the ocean.

8. Festas e Traditions: Celebrations of Culture: Immerse yourself in Vila do Corvo's festivals, where local traditions, music, and dance come together to celebrate the island's vibrant cultural heritage.

9. Sunset Serenade at Ponta Negra: Nature's Farewell: Witness the sun's serene descent from Ponta Negra, where the horizon becomes a canvas of colors, bidding a tranquil farewell to the day.

10. Vila do Corvo's Timeless Charm: A Memory Forever Treasured: Vila do Corvo's timeless charm creates a memory forever treasured, where each moment allows you to embrace nature's untouched beauty and find solace in the island's intimate allure.

Vila do Corvo is a haven of tranquility and natural splendor, where the simplicity of life intertwines with the magnificence of nature. From historic squares to panoramic views, from coastal vistas to cultural celebrations, the village welcomes you to explore, immerse, and create memories that will forever resonate in your heart.

2.9 Which Islands to Visit and Why

With nine captivating islands to explore, Each island has its unique charm and attractions, and choosing where to visit might seem like a delightful challenge. Let's embark on a journey to help you discover which islands are right for you, that resonate with your interests and preferences.

1. São Miguel: The Emerald Gem: Visit São Miguel, the largest island, for its lush landscapes, vibrant culture, and bustling city life. Explore its stunning crater lakes, immerse in hot springs, and experience the charm of Ponta Delgada.

2. Terceira: History and Festivities: Experience the historical charm of Terceira, with its UNESCO-listed city of Angra do Heroísmo and vibrant festivals like Sanjoaninas.

Explore volcanic landscapes and discover the Algar do Carvão lava cave.

3. Faial: Nautical Wonders: Choose Faial for its maritime heritage and stunning landscapes. Sailors' traditions are alive in Horta's marina, and the Caldeira crater offers breathtaking views. Don't miss Capelinhos, a volcanic landscape that emerged from the sea.

4. Pico: Majestic Peaks and Vineyards: Conquer Pico's majestic peak, Montanha do Pico, and explore its unique vineyards, recognized by UNESCO. Dive into its underwater world and embrace the island's rich maritime history.

5. São Jorge: Dramatic Cliffs and Tradition: São Jorge beckons with its dramatic cliffs, traditional windmills, and lush landscapes. Discover Fajãs, coastal flatlands, and immerse in a cultural tapestry woven with stories.

6. Graciosa: Tranquility and Volcanic Marvels: For tranquility and volcanic marvels, visit Graciosa. Explore Furna do Enxofre's cave, relax in natural pools, and savor local flavors amidst the charming streets of Santa Cruz.

7. Flores: Nature's Palette and Serenity: Uncover Flores' natural wonders, from colorful lakes to cascading waterfalls. Marvel at Rocha dos Bordões' basalt formations and embrace a sense of serenity on this untouched island.

8. Corvo: Remote Paradise and Solitude: For a truly remote experience, Corvo awaits untouched landscapes and a sense of solitude. Witness Caldeirão's volcanic marvel and immerse in the simplicity of Vila do Corvo.

Here's a simple tip to help you:
Ultimately, the best island to visit in the Azores depends on your interests and preferences. If you are looking for stunning scenery, São Miguel and Terceira are great options. If you are interested in whale watching, Pico and Faial

are good choices. And if you are looking for a laid-back atmosphere, Flores and Corvo are perfect.

Each island in the Azores is a world of its own, a symphony of landscapes and culture waiting to be explored. Whether you're drawn to active adventures, cultural riches, or tranquil escapes, the Azores offers an array of choices that promise to make your journey unforgettable.

CHAPTER 3

Top Attractions & Activities

3.1 Natural Wonders and Landscapes

If you're a nature lover, you'll fall in love with the Azores. This stunning archipelago in the Atlantic Ocean boasts breathtaking landscapes that are sure to take your breath away. The rugged coastlines, lush forests, and stunning volcanic craters make it a paradise for hikers, bird watchers, and wildlife enthusiasts.

With a variety of unique flora and fauna, the Azores is a popular destination for those seeking to immerse themselves in nature. Whether you're looking to explore majestic mountains, soak in hot springs, or simply relax on beautiful beaches, the Azores has something for everyone.

Here are a list of them:

3.1.1 Sete Cidades Crater Lakes

As a traveler drawn to the wonders of the Azores archipelago, there's an enchanting gem awaiting your discovery on São Miguel. The Sete Cidades Crater Lakes, a natural wonder that transcends the imagination, beckon you to experience the breathtaking fusion of color and beauty that defines this mesmerizing destination.

- **Sete Cidades: A Spectacular Canvas Unveiled:** Imagine standing before the Sete Cidades Crater Lakes, where nature has wielded its artistic brush to craft a spectacle beyond words. Before you lie the Blue Lake and Green Lake, their waters mirroring the ever-changing sky in an extraordinary dance of colors. The Blue Lake's deep cerulean shade stretches infinitely, while the Green

Lake's vibrant emerald hues paint a scene of unparalleled beauty.

- **A Legend-Born Landscape:** Digging deeper into the experience, you'll uncover the legend that lends an air of magic to these lakes. Local tales speak of a blue-eyed princess and a shepherd with green eyes, their forbidden love giving rise to these contrasting lakes. As you gaze upon their waters, the story takes on a tangible presence, adding a layer of enchantment to your visit.
- **Embracing Panoramic Splendor:** For an unparalleled perspective, venture to the miradouros, the viewpoints that grace the surrounding hills. From these elevated vantage points, you'll witness the Sete Cidades Crater Lakes in their full splendor. The undulating hills that frame the lakes and the picturesque

landscape create a scene that's both captivating and serene.

- **Uniqueness:** Sete Cidades is a unique and beautiful place that is worth visiting. The two-colored lakes are a sight to see, as is the surrounding countryside.
- **Location:** Sete Cidades is located in the western part of the island of Sao Miguel. It is about a 30-minute drive from the capital, Ponta Delgada.
- **Reaching the Crater Lakes: The Best Path:** There are ways to get to Sete Cidades. You can drive, take a bus, or go on a guided tour. To reach this nature's masterpiece, set your course to the picturesque town of Sete Cidades. A winding road leads to the Miradouro da Vista do Rei, offering a breathtaking initial view of the lakes from above. For a closer encounter, the road descends to the lakes' shores, where you can wander

along the trails that offer a closer connection to this natural marvel.

- **Operating hours:** Sete Cidades is open 24 hours a day. The ideal times to visit, however, are early in the morning or late in the afternoon, when the crowds are lighter.
- **Admission fees:** There is no admission fee to visit Sete Cidades, however, there is a parking fee of €2 per hour.

Your visit to the Sete Cidades Crater Lakes is more than sightseeing; it's an immersion into the raw beauty of the Azores. As you witness the interplay of sunlight and water during sunrise or sunset, a sense of wonder and connection washes over you. The Sete Cidades Crater Lakes stand as an invitation to experience the magic of nature and the captivating allure that the Azores' landscapes offer to explorers like you.

3.1.2 Furnas Hot Springs

The Furnas Hot Springs is a truly unique natural wonder and a must-visit for any visitor to the Azores. With their stunning scenery, hot springs, and geothermal activity, the Furnas Hot Springs is sure to leave a lasting impression. It's a popular tourist destination and offers a variety of activities for visitors to enjoy. Visitors can swim in the hot springs, bathe in the mud pools, and cook their food in the geothermal ovens. The springs are also home to a variety of wildlife, including turtles, ducks, and frogs.

- **Location:** The Furnas Hot Springs are located in the Furnas caldera on the island of São Miguel. The caldera is about 10 kilometers (6.2 miles) in diameter and is surrounded by mountains.
- **How to Get There:** The Furnas Hot Springs are easily accessible by car. There is a parking lot near the springs

where visitors can park their cars. There are also a few buses that run from the city of Ponta Delgada to Furnas.
- **Operating Hours:** The Furnas Hot Springs is open year-round. The hours vary depending on the season, but they are generally open from 9 am to 7 pm.
- **Admission Fees:** The admission fee to the Furnas Hot Springs is €5 for adults and €3 for children. There is also an additional parking fee.

For a truly transformative experience, consider indulging in the thermal waters, their mineral content is believed to hold therapeutic properties.

In the heart of the Azores, the Furnas Hot Springs beckon as a natural wonder that bridges the gap between Earth's fiery depths and the surface world.

3.1.3 Lagoa do Fogo

Lagoa do Fogo is a volcanic crater lake located on the island of São Miguel in the Azores. It is the second-largest lake in the Azores and is surrounded by lush green hills and black lava rocks. The lake is fed by rainwater and melting snow from the surrounding mountains. The name Lagoa do Fogo means "Lake of Fire" in Portuguese. This name is thought to come from the fact that the lake was formed by a volcanic eruption in 1563. The eruption created a caldera, which is a bowl-shaped depression that is formed when a volcano collapses.

The lake was filled with rainwater and melted snow, creating the beautiful lake that we see today. Lagoa do Fogo is a popular tourist destination and offers a variety of activities for visitors to enjoy. Visitors can hike to the rim of the crater, swim in the lake, and go boating. Bird viewing is very popular around the lake.

- **Location:** Lagoa do Fogo is located in the western part of the island of São Miguel. It is about a 45-minute drive from the capital city of Ponta Delgada.
- **How to Get There:** The best way to get to Lagoa do Fogo is by car. There is a parking lot near the lake where visitors can park their cars. There are also a few buses that run from Ponta Delgada to Lagoa do Fogo.
- **Operating Hours:** Lagoa do Fogo is open year-round. The ideal seasons to visit are spring and autumn when the temperature is warm.
- **Admission Fees:** There is no admission fee to visit Lagoa do Fogo. However, there is a parking fee of €2 per car.

Lagoa do Fogo is a truly unique natural wonder and a must-visit for any visitor to the Azores. With its stunning scenery, volcanic crater lake, and lush green hills, Lagoa do Fogo is sure to leave a lasting impression. Standing before Lagoa do Fogo, you'll feel a deep connection to the Azorean landscape and the earth's innate beauty. Whether you're capturing the vista with your camera or simply absorbing the tranquility, this natural wonder leaves an indelible mark on your soul. The journey to Lagoa do Fogo is a testament to the Azores' gift for revealing nature's most treasured moments, inviting you to bask in the splendor and create memories that last a lifetime.

3.1.4 Pico Mountain

Pico Mountain is a natural wonder located in the Azores archipelago. It is the highest mountain in Portugal and the second-highest volcanic peak in the Atlantic Ocean. The mountain is about 2,351 meters (7,713 feet) tall and is located on the island of Pico.

Pico Mountain is a UNESCO World Heritage Site and is known for its unique volcanic landscape. The mountain is covered in craters, lava fields, and cinder cones. Many hiking trails lead to the summit of the mountain, offering stunning views of the surrounding islands.

- **Uniqueness:** Pico Mountain is unique in many ways. It is the highest mountain in Portugal and the second-highest volcanic peak in the Atlantic Ocean. It is also the only mountain in the Azores that has been designated as a UNESCO World Heritage Site. Additionally, Pico Mountain is home to many endemic species of plants and animals, making it an important biodiversity hotspot.
- **Location:** Pico Mountain is located on the island of Pico in the Azores archipelago. The island is about 400 kilometers (250 miles) west of Portugal.

- **How to Get There:** The best way to get to Pico Mountain is by plane. Many airlines fly to the island of Pico from Portugal and other European countries. Once on the island, you can take a taxi or bus to the town of Madalena, which is the closest town to the mountain. From Madalena, you can hike or take a cable car to the summit of the mountain.
- **Operating Hours:** The cable car to the summit of Pico Mountain is open year-round. The hours vary depending on the season, but they are generally open from 9 am to 5 pm.
- **Admission Fees:** The admission fee to the cable car to the summit of Pico Mountain is €25 for adults and €15 for children. There is also an additional parking fee.

Tips for Visiting:

- Pico Mountain can get crowded, especially during the summer months. If you are planning on visiting, it is best to go early in the morning or later in the afternoon.
- Wear comfortable shoes as you will be doing a lot of hiking.
- Bring a jacket as it can get cold at the summit of the mountain.
- Be careful not to get too close to the edge of the craters as it can be dangerous.

Pico Mountain is a truly unique natural wonder and a must-visit for any visitor to the Azores. With its stunning scenery, volcanic landscape, and endemic species, Pico Mountain is sure to leave a lasting impression. Pico Mountain stands not just as a towering peak but as a symbol of the Azores' captivating beauty and geological history. The ascent to its summit is a journey that brings you closer to nature's raw forces, offering a sense of accomplishment and panoramic views that linger in memory. This natural wonder invites you to explore the harmonious interplay of earth and sky, leaving an indelible mark on your Azorean adventure.

3.1.5 Algar do Carvão

Algar do Carvão is a natural wonder located in the Azores archipelago. It is a lava tube cave that is about 90 meters (295 feet) deep and 500 meters (1,640 feet) long. The cave was formed by a volcanic eruption about 3,200 years ago.

Algar do Carvo translates to "Coal Cave" in Portuguese. This name is thought to come from the fact that the cave was once used to mine coal. However, the coal deposits have since been depleted.

Algar do Carvão is a unique natural wonder for many reasons. It is one of the few lava tube caves in the Azores that is open to the public. Additionally, the cave is home to many stalactites and stalagmites, making it a popular tourist destination.

- **Location:** Algar do Carvão is located on the island of Terceira in the Azores archipelago. The cave is about a 20-minute drive from the town of Angra do Heroísmo, the capital of the island.
- **How to Get There:** The best way to get to Algar do Carvão is by car. There is a parking lot near the cave where visitors can park their cars. There are also a few buses that run from Angra do Heroísmo to Algar do Carvão.
- **Operating Hours:** Algar do Carvão is open year-round. The hours vary depending on the season, but they are generally open from 9 am to 5 pm.

- **Admission Fees:** The admission fee to Algar do Carvão is €5 for adults and €3 for children. In addition, there is a parking cost.

Algar do Carvão can get crowded, especially during the summer months. If you are planning on visiting, it is best to go early in the morning or later in the afternoon. Bring a flashlight as it can get dark in the cave. Be careful not to touch the stalactites and stalagmites as they can be fragile.

Algar do Carvão is a truly unique natural wonder and a must-visit for any visitor to the Azores. With its stunning scenery, lava tube cave, stalactites, and stalagmites. Algar do Carvão invites you to venture beyond the surface and witness the Earth's inner secrets. Its unique formations, illuminated by natural light, create a mesmerizing experience that connects you to the island's volcanic origins. As you explore the cavern's depths, you're reminded of the incredible forces that have shaped the Azores' landscapes, leaving you in awe of nature's creative power.

3.2 Outdoor Adventures

3.2.1 Hiking and Trekking in the Azores

The Azores is a great destination for hikers and trekkers. The islands offer a variety of trails for all levels of experience, from easy walks through the countryside to challenging hikes up volcanic mountains.

Here are a few of the most popular hiking and trekking routes in the Azores:

- **Sete Cidades trek:** This moderate 6.4-kilometer (4-mile) looped trail takes you around the Sete Cidades caldera, one of the most scenic spots in the Azores.

You'll pass by two beautiful crater lakes, lush forests, and waterfalls.

- **Lagoa do Fogo hike:** This challenging 8.4-kilometer (5.2 miles) out-and-back trail takes you to the top of Mount Fogo, the second-highest mountain in the Azores. The views from the summit are incredible, and you can even see the neighboring islands of Faial and Pico on a clear day.
- **Pico Mountain hike:** This strenuous 10-kilometer (6.2 miles) out-and-back trail takes you to the summit of Pico Mountain, the highest mountain in Portugal. The hike is challenging, but the views from the summit are worth it. You can see the neighboring islands of Faial, São Jorge, and Graciosa on a clear day.
- **Caldeira Velha hike:** This easy 1.6-kilometer (1 mile) looped trail takes you through the lush rainforest to the

Caldeira Velha geothermal park. You can bathe in the natural hot springs and see the fumaroles and geysers.

- **Furnas hike:** This moderate 4.8-kilometer (3-mile) looped trail takes you through the Furnas caldera, a volcanic crater that is home to several hot springs, geysers, and fumaroles. You can also see the Terra Nostra Botanical Garden, which is home to a variety of plants from around the world.

These are just a few of the many great hiking and trekking routes in the Azores. Whatever your skill level or interests are, you're likely to discover a route that's right for you.

Tips for Hiking and Trekking in the Azores:

- Wear hiking shoes that are comfortable and acceptable.
- Bring plenty of water and snacks.

- Even on foggy days, use sunscreen and a hat.
- Be mindful of the weather and dress decently.
- Tell someone where you're going and when you anticipate to return.
- Be respectful of the environment and wildlife.
- Local guides are available to enhance your experience with their knowledge of the terrain and local anecdotes.

Hiking and trekking in the Azores is more than a physical journey; it's a chance to connect with the islands' soul-stirring landscapes. Whether you're drawn to coastal vistas, volcanic wonders, forest retreats, or lakeside tranquility, the Azores' outdoor adventures offer an intimate exploration of nature's wonders that will leave an indelible mark on your heart.

3.2.2 Whale Watching in the Azores

The Azores are a great destination for whale watching. The islands are located in the middle of the Atlantic Ocean, which is a major migration route for whales and dolphins.

Here are a few of the most common whales and dolphins that you can see on a whale-watching tour in the Azores:

Blue whales are the biggest mammals on the planet, reaching lengths of up to 100 feet. They are filter feeders and eat small crustaceans and krill.

- **Fin whales:** Fin whales are the second-largest animals on Earth and can grow up to 80 feet long. They are also filter feeders and eat small crustaceans and krill.
- **Sei whales:** Sei whales are smaller than blue and fin whales, but they are still quite large and can grow up to 60 feet

long. They are also filter feeders and eat small crustaceans and krill.

- **Humpback whales:** Humpback whales are known for their acrobatic behavior and can breach the water, lobtail, and spy hop. They are also filter feeders and eat small crustaceans and krill.
- **Orcas:** Orcas are also known as killer whales and are apex predators. They eat a variety of marine animals, including fish, seals, and dolphins.
- **Dolphins:** Several species of dolphins can be seen on whale-watching tours in the Azores, including sperm whales, pilot whales, and bottlenose dolphins.

Whale watching in the Azores is a great way to see these amazing creatures in their natural habitat. It is also a great way to learn about the importance of protecting these animals and their environment.

Tips for Whale Watching in the Azores:

- Go on a tour with a reputable company that has experienced captains and crew.
- Dress in layers so that you can adjust to the temperature changes.
- Bring binoculars so that you can get a closer look at the whales and dolphins.
- Be patient and respectful of the whales and dolphins.
- Be prepared to get wet!

Whale watching in the Azores is a unique opportunity to connect with the ocean's most majestic inhabitants and witness the magic of marine life in its natural habitat. The experience is not only a thrilling adventure but also a reminder of the importance of preserving and protecting these awe-inspiring creatures and the oceans they call home.

3.2.3 Scuba Diving in the Azores

The Azores are an excellent scuba diving location. The islands are located in the middle of the Atlantic Ocean, which has some of the clearest waters in the world. This makes it possible to see marine life up close, even at depths of 100 feet or more.

Here are a few of the things you can see while scuba diving in the Azores:

- **Wrecks:** Several shipwrecks can be explored while scuba diving in the Azores, including the SS Santa Maria, a British cargo ship that sank in 1968.
- **Coral reefs:** The Azores have a variety of coral reefs, including hard and soft corals, sponges, and anemones.
- **Marine life:** The Azores are home to a variety of marine life, including fish, sharks, turtles, and dolphins.

- **Blue holes:** Blue holes are underwater sinkholes that are popular for scuba diving. They are often home to a variety of marine life, including sharks and rays.

Scuba diving in the Azores is a great way to see these amazing creatures in their natural habitat. It is also a great way to learn about the importance of protecting these animals and their environment.

Tips for Scuba Diving in the Azores:
- Go on a tour with a reputable company that has experienced divemasters.
- Make sure you are certified to the appropriate level for the dives you want to do.
- Bring the right equipment, including a wetsuit, mask, fins, and a buoyancy compensator.
- Be prepared for the cold water, even in the summer months.

- Respect the ecosystem and aquatic life.

Scuba diving in the Azores is an opportunity to unlock a world of underwater magic and exploration. Whether you're a seasoned diver or a novice, the archipelago's diverse marine environments promise a journey into the heart of the ocean's secrets, creating memories that will forever linger in your mind and heart.

3.2.4 Surfing and Watersports in the Azores

The Azores is a great destination for surfing and watersports. The islands have a mild climate and consistent swells, making them perfect for a variety of water activities.

Here are a few of the best places to surf in the Azores:

- **Praia da Vitória:** This beach on the island of Terceira is known for its long, rolling waves. It is an excellent location for both novice and expert surfers.

- **Santa Cruz:** This beach on the island of São Miguel is known for its powerful waves. It is a great place for experienced surfers.
- **Praia da Ribeira Seca:** This beach on the island of Pico is known for its consistent waves. It is a great place for all levels of surfers.

In addition to surfing, there are a variety of other watersports that can be enjoyed in the Azores, including:

- **Kitesurfing:** Kitesurfing is a great way to explore the coastline of the Azores. It is a demanding sport, but it is also quite rewarding.
- **Windsurfing:** Windsurfing is similar to kitesurfing, but it is powered by the wind instead of a kite. It is a great way to get exercise and enjoy the scenery.

- **Stand-up paddleboarding:** Stand-up paddleboarding is a great way to get around the islands and explore the coastline. It is also a great workout.

Surfing and watersports in the Azores are great ways to get active and enjoy the natural beauty of the islands. With their consistent swells and mild climate, the Azores are a perfect destination for water lovers of all levels.

Tips for Surfing and Watersports in the Azores:

- Go on a tour with a reputable company that has experienced instructors.
- Check that you have the appropriate equipment for the situation.
- Be prepared for the cold water, even in the summer months.
- Respect the ecosystem and aquatic life.
- Professional instructors and guides ensure safety while promoting

responsible and eco-conscious practices that protect the marine ecosystem.

Surfing, paddleboarding, and kayaking in the Azores offer a captivating way to connect with the ocean's boundless energy. Whether you're riding the waves, paddling along tranquil shores, or encountering marine life up close, the watersports scene promises an immersion into the Azores' natural splendor that will resonate long after the adventure ends.

3.3 Cultural and Historical Sites

3.3.1 Angra do Heroísmo Historic Center

The Historic Center of Angra do Heroísmo is a UNESCO World Heritage Site located on the island of Terceira in the Azores. The city was founded in 1478 and was the capital of the Azores from 1583 to 1766.

The historic center is well-preserved and is a great example of Portuguese colonial architecture. The streets are lined with pastel-colored houses, churches, and government buildings. The city also has many museums, including the Angra do Heroísmo Museum, which houses a collection of artifacts from the city's history.

Here are a few of the things you can see and do in the Historic Center of Angra do Heroísmo:

- **Visit the Sé Catedral de Angra do Heroísmo:** This cathedral was built in the 16th century and is the oldest cathedral in the Azores.
- **Explore the city's narrow streets:** The streets of the historic center are lined with pastel-colored houses and shops. It's an excellent area to get lost and walk about.

- **Visit the Angra do Heroísmo Museum:** This museum houses a collection of artifacts from the city's history, including furniture, paintings, and sculptures.
- **Take a stroll around the waterfront:** The waterfront is a terrific area to unwind and enjoy the harbor views. There are also many restaurants and cafes where you can enjoy a meal or a drink.

The Historic Center of Angra do Heroísmo is a beautiful and historic city that is a great place to visit for a day or two. It is a UNESCO World Heritage Site for a reason, and it is sure to impress visitors with its well-preserved architecture and rich history.

Tips for Visiting the Historic Center of Angra do Heroísmo:
- Allow at least a day to explore the city.
- Wear comfy shoes since you will be walking a lot.

- Bring a camera to capture the city's splendor.
- Be respectful of the city's history and heritage.

Angra do Heroísmo Historic Center is more than a collection of buildings; it's a living tapestry of stories, traditions, and the enduring spirit of a community. As you meander through its streets, you'll find yourself not only immersed in history but also connected to the essence of the Azores, where the past and present coexist in perfect harmony.

3.3.2 The Capelinhos Volcano Interpretation Center

The Capelinhos Volcano Interpretation Center is a cultural and historical site located on the island of Faial in the Azores. The center was built in 1974 to commemorate the eruption of the Capelinhos volcano, which began in September 1957 and lasted for 13 months.

The Capelinhos volcano is one of the most recent volcanoes to erupt in the Azores. The eruption destroyed the village of Vila Nova do Capelo, which was located on the cape that gave the volcano its name. The eruption also created a new peninsula, which is now home to the Capelinhos Volcano Interpretation Center.

The center is built on the site of the old village of Vila Nova do Capelo. The center houses a museum that exhibits artifacts from the eruption, as well as many interactive exhibits that teach visitors about volcanoes and the Capelinhos eruption. The center also has a viewing platform that offers stunning views of the crater of the Capelinhos volcano.

Here are a few of the things you can see and do at the Capelinhos Volcano Interpretation Center:

- **Visit the museum:** The museum exhibits artifacts from the eruption, as well as many interactive exhibits that teach visitors about volcanoes and the Capelinhos eruption.

- **Take a walk along the lava field:** The lava field that was created by the eruption is now home to a variety of plants and animals. It's a great place to go for a walk and explore the natural beauty of the area.
- **Visit the viewing platform:** The viewing platform offers stunning views of the crater of the Capelinhos volcano. It's a great place to take pictures and enjoy the scenery.

The Capelinhos Volcano Interpretation Center is a unique cultural and historical site that is a great place to learn about the history of the Azores and the power of volcanoes. It is a must-visit for anyone interested in volcanoes or the natural beauty of the Azores.

Tips for Visiting the Capelinhos Volcano Interpretation Center:

- Allow at least a few hours to explore the center.
- Wear comfy shoes since you will be walking a lot.
- Bring a camera to capture the area's splendor.
- Be respectful of the natural environment.

The Capelinhos Volcano Interpretation Center is a journey into the heart of Faial's past, where the forces of nature have left an indelible mark. As you explore this unique site, you'll not only gain insight into the Azores' geological evolution but also admire the resilience of the human spirit in the face of adversity—a testament to the enduring bond between the islands and their inhabitants.

3.3.3 Museu Carlos Machado

The Museu Carlos Machado is a cultural and historical site located in the city of Ponta Delgada on the island of São Miguel in the Azores. The museum was founded in 1876 by Carlos Machado, a Portuguese doctor and naturalist.

The museum houses a collection of artifacts that showcase the history and culture of the Azores. The collection includes exhibits on geology, archaeology, ethnography, and fine arts. There is also a library and a research center in the museum.

Here are a few of the things you can see and do at the Museu Carlos Machado:

- **Visit the geology exhibit**: The geology exhibit showcases the volcanic history of the Azores.
- **See the archaeological artifacts:** The archaeological artifacts showcase

artifacts from the prehistoric and historic periods of the Azores.

- **Learn about the traditional culture of the Azores:** The ethnography exhibit showcases the traditional culture of the Azores, including clothing, furniture, and tools.
- **Enjoy the fine arts:** The fine arts exhibit showcases paintings, sculptures, and other works of art from the Azores and Portugal.

The Museu Carlos Machado is a great place to learn about the history and culture of the Azores. It is a must-visit for anyone interested in the Azores or Portuguese culture.

Tips for Visiting the Museu Carlos Machado:

- Allow several hours to tour the museum.
- Wear comfy shoes since you will be walking a lot.
- Bring a camera to capture the exhibitions' splendor.

- Be respectful of the artifacts and the museum's staff.

The Museu Carlos Machado beckons visitors to immerse themselves in the rich mosaic of Azorean history and culture. Through its exhibits, artifacts, and artistic treasures, the museum offers a profound connection to the past and a deeper understanding of the Azores' enduring spirit—a cultural journey that resonates far beyond its walls.

3.4 Local Cuisine and Food Experiences

3.4.1 Traditional Dishes and Restaurants

The islands have a rich culinary tradition, with dishes that reflect the region's Portuguese, African, and Brazilian influences.

Here are a few of the most popular traditional dishes in the Azores:

- **Cozido das Furnas:** This stew is cooked in underground ovens called Furnas. The ingredients typically include beef, pork, chicken, sausage, potatoes, carrots, and cabbage.
- **Arroz de lapas:** This rice dish is made with limpets, a type of shellfish. The limpets are cooked in a tomato sauce with rice and spices.
- **Pastel de nata:** This custard tart is a Portuguese classic. The tart is made with a flaky pastry crust and a rich custard filling.
- **Alcatra:** This beef stew is a popular dish on the island of Terceira. The beef is cooked in a red wine sauce with potatoes, carrots, and onions.
- **Queijada da Ilha:** This is a traditional cheese tart from the island of São Jorge.

The tart is made with a sweet pastry crust and a filling of fresh cheese, eggs, and sugar.

Here are a few of the best restaurants in the Azores to try these traditional dishes:

- **Adega da Avó:** This restaurant in Ponta Delgada is a great place to try cozido das furnas.
- **Taberna da Quinta:** This restaurant in Furnas is a great place to try alcatra.
- **Cavalheiro:** This restaurant in Ponta Delgada is a great place to try pastel de nata.
- **Café Sport:** This restaurant in Angra do Heroísmo is a great place to try queijada da ilha.

The Azores are a great place to experience the local cuisine. With their fresh seafood, traditional dishes, and delicious pastries, the islands are sure to tantalize your taste buds.

Exploring traditional dishes and restaurants in the Azores is a voyage of flavor and culture. Each bite transports you to the heart of Azorean life, offering a taste of the island's history, traditions, and the warmth of its people. Savoring Azorean cuisine is not just about nourishing the body; it's about indulging in the spirit of the archipelago and creating memories that linger long after the meal is over.

3.4.2 Wine Tasting

The islands are known for their stunning scenery, volcanic lakes, and friendly locals. But did you know that the Azores are also home to some of the best wines in Portugal?

Winemaking has been practiced in the Azores since the 15th century. The islands' volcanic soil and climate are ideal for growing grapes, and the local winemakers produce a variety of wines, including red, white, and rosé.

If you're looking for a unique wine-tasting experience, the Azores are the perfect destination.

Here are a few of the best places to go wine tasting in the Azores:

- **Biscoitos Wine Estate:** This estate on the island of Pico is home to some of the best wines in the Azores. The estate offers a variety of wine-tasting experiences, including tours of the vineyards and cellars.
- **Terra Nostra Botanical Garden:** This garden on the island of São Miguel has a vineyard and a wine cellar. Visitors can enjoy a wine tasting in the garden, surrounded by stunning scenery.
- **Quinta da Graciosa:** This winery on the island of Graciosa offers a variety of wine-tasting experiences, including tours of the vineyards and cellars. The winery

also has a restaurant where you can enjoy a meal paired with wine.

No matter where you go wine tasting in the Azores, you're sure to enjoy the delicious wines and the stunning scenery. So raise a glass and toast to the Azores!

Here are some additional tips for wine tasting in the Azores:

- **Visit during the harvest season (September-October).** This is the best time to see the vineyards and taste the freshest wines.
- **Go with a local guide.** They can help you choose the right wines and explain the winemaking process.
- **Sample a variety of wines.** The Azores produce a variety of wines, so be sure to try a few different ones.
- **Pair your wines with food.** The Azores have delicious cuisine, so be sure to pair your wines with local dishes.

- **Enjoy the experience!** Wine tasting in the Azores is a great way to relax and enjoy the local culture.

Wine tasting in the Azores is a voyage of the senses, an exploration of the islands' unique viticultural landscape. With each sip, you're not only tasting the flavors of the region but also immersing yourself in a tradition that spans generations—an experience that leaves an indelible mark on your palate and your heart.

3.4.3 Local Markets in the Azores

The islands are known for their stunning scenery, volcanic lakes, and friendly locals. But did you know that the Azores are also home to a variety of local markets?

Local markets are a great place to experience the local cuisine and culture of the Azores. Visitors can find fresh produce, locally made cheeses, and traditional handicrafts at the markets. They are also a great place to meet locals and learn about the islands' history and way of life.

Here are a few of the best local markets in the Azores:

- **Mercado da Graça:** This market in Ponta Delgada, on the island of São Miguel, is the largest and most popular market in the Azores. Except on Sunday, it is open every day and is a great place to find fresh produce, meats, cheeses, and other local products.
- **Mercado da Ribeira Grande:** This market in Ribeira Grande, on the island of São Miguel, is a smaller market that is open every day except Sunday. It is a great place to find fresh fish, locally made pastries, and other local delicacies.
- **Mercado da Horta:** This market in Horta, on the island of Faial, is a great place to find fresh seafood, locally made

wines, and other regional products.

Except on Sunday, it is open every day. No matter which market you choose to visit, you're sure to find something delicious to eat and something unique to take home with you. So next time you're in the Azores, be sure to check out a local market and experience the islands' flavors for yourself!

Here are some additional tips for visiting local markets in the Azores:

- **Arrive early:** The markets are busiest in the morning, so it's best to arrive early to get the best selection of products.
- **Be prepared to haggle:** It's customary to haggle at local markets in the Azores. So don't be scared to bargain.
- **Sample the local produce:** Many of the stalls at the markets will offer samples of their products. So be sure to try a few things before you buy.

- **Support local businesses:** When you shop at local markets, you're supporting local businesses and the local economy. So make sure to pick up a few souvenirs to take home with you.
- **Enjoy the experience:** Local markets are a great way to experience the local culture and cuisine of the Azores. So sit back, take your time, and enjoy the ride!

Local markets in the Azores encapsulate the essence of the island's culinary culture—a fusion of nature's bounty and the warmth of the local community. As you wander through the colorful stalls, you're not just shopping; you're immersing yourself in a tradition that celebrates the connection between the land, the sea, and the people. It's an invitation to experience the Azores through your taste buds and take a flavorful piece of the islands with you wherever you go.

CHAPTER 4

Accommodation Options

4.1 Hotels and Resorts

The Azores is a great destination for a relaxing vacation, and there are many excellent hotels and resorts to choose from. Here are a few of the best hotels and resorts in the Azores, with their prices per night:

- **The Reid's Palace, São Miguel Island:** This luxurious hotel is located in the capital city of Ponta Delgada. It has a spa, a golf course, and several restaurants. Prices start at \$600 per night.
- **Ponta dos Gatos, São Miguel Island:** This boutique hotel is located on a cliff overlooking the ocean. It has a

swimming pool, a hot tub, and a restaurant. Prices start at \$300 per night.

- **Terra Nostra Garden Hotel & Spa, São Miguel Island:** This hotel is located in the Terra Nostra Botanical Garden. Nestled on São Miguel Island, the Terra Nostra Garden Hotel is a true gem. Immerse yourself in the tranquility of its historic charm, where a magnificent botanical garden and therapeutic thermal pools invite relaxation. With prices starting at approximately $200 per night, this luxurious haven offers a harmonious union of opulence and natural splendor. It has a spa and several restaurants.
- **Furnas Boutique Hotel:** Embracing the idyllic Furnas Valley, the Furnas Boutique Hotel marries modern elegance with Azorean tradition. Delight in the healing power of thermal waters at its spa, indulge in gourmet dining and soak

in sweeping vistas of volcanic landscapes. Starting at around $180 per night, this distinctive retreat promises an exquisite blend of serenity and sophistication.

- **Santa Bárbara Eco-Beach Resort:** On the northern coast of São Miguel, the Santa Bárbara Eco-Beach Resort beckons nature enthusiasts. Gaze upon the vast ocean and be enveloped by verdant surroundings, all while indulging in modern luxury with eco-conscious practices. With rates beginning at around $160 per night, this resort offers an eco-friendly haven for the conscious traveler.

- **Hotel Quinta da Rosa, Faial Island:** This hotel is located in the countryside on the island of Faial. It has a swimming pool, a tennis court, and a restaurant. Prices start at \$150 per night.

- **São Vicente Lodge:** For a boutique experience that embodies the spirit of Terceira Island, the São Vicente Lodge is a captivating choice. With stylish design, personalized service, and proximity to historical sites, it offers an authentic Azorean escape. Starting at about $100 per night, this lodge is an accessible gateway to the island's charm and allure.
- **Hotel do Canal, Pico Island:** This hotel is located in the town of Madalena on the island of Pico. There is a swimming pool, bar and restaurant. Prices start at \$100 per night.
- **Charming Azorean Houses:** Immerse yourself in the local lifestyle by opting for charming guesthouses and traditional houses for rent. From cozy cottages to quaint village abodes, prices vary based on location and amenities, starting at approximately $70 per night. These

unique accommodations provide an authentic way to embrace the Azorean culture and way of life.

These are just a few of the many great hotels and resorts in the Azores. When choosing a hotel, it is important to consider your budget and your desired location. The Azores have something to offer everyone, so you're sure to find the perfect place to stay.

Here are some additional tips for choosing accommodation in the Azores:

- **Book your hotel in advance:** The Azores are a popular tourist destination, so it is important to book your hotel in advance, especially if you are traveling during the peak season (June-September).
- **Consider your budget:** The Azores have a wide range of accommodation options, from luxury resorts to

budget-friendly guesthouses. Decide how much you are willing to spend on accommodation before you start your search.

- **Think about your desired location:** The Azores are made up of nine islands, each with its unique charm. Decide which island you want to visit and choose a hotel that is located in a convenient location.
- **Read reviews:** Before you book your hotel, be sure to read reviews from other travelers. This will help you get a sense of what to expect from your stay.
- **Be flexible:** If you are not able to get your desired hotel, be flexible with your dates or your location. There are many great hotels in the Azores, so you are sure to find one that you love.

In the Azores, where nature's beauty knows no bounds, the accommodations are no less remarkable. From opulent resorts to charming lodgings, each option invites you to cocoon yourself in the embrace of the archipelago's allure. Whether you seek luxury, authenticity, or a combination of both, the Azores' hospitality ensures an unforgettable stay that mirrors the islands' splendor.

4.2 Guesthouses and Bed & Breakfasts

Here are some of the best guesthouses and bed and breakfasts in the Azores with their prices per night:

- **Quinta da Alagoa, São Miguel Island:** This guesthouse is located in the countryside on the island of São Miguel. It has a swimming pool, a garden, and a barbecue area. Prices start at \$100 per night.

- **Solar da Glória ao Carmo:** On Terceira Island, Solar da Glória ao Carmo stands as a testament to Azorean history. This historic mansion-turned-guesthouse offers elegant accommodations, antique charm, and a central location. Starting at approximately $100 per night, it's a window into the island's past and present.
- **Casa do Pico, Pico Island:** This bed and breakfast is located in the town of Madalena on the island of Pico. It has a garden, a terrace, and a shared kitchen. Prices start at \$80 per night.
- **Quinta da Terça:** Nestled on São Miguel Island, Quinta da Terça is a charming escape. This historic property offers elegantly restored rooms, lush gardens, and a tranquil atmosphere. With prices starting at around $80 per night,

it's a budget-friendly way to experience Azorean hospitality in a serene setting.

- **Herdade do Ananas, São Miguel Island:** This guesthouse is located in the countryside on the island of São Miguel. It has a pineapple plantation, a swimming pool, and a garden. Prices start at \$90 per night.
- **Casa da Tia Maria, Terceira Island:** This bed and breakfast is located in the town of Angra do Heroísmo on the island of Terceira. It has a garden, a terrace, and a shared kitchen. Prices start at \$70 per night.
- **Quinta do Martelo:** Located on Terceira Island, Quinta do Martelo enchants with its traditional Azorean architecture and inviting atmosphere. It provides a tranquil hideaway surrounded by lovely landscapes. Starting at about $70 per night, this bed & breakfast is an

affordable option that doesn't compromise on comfort.
- **Guesthouse São Jorge, São Jorge Island:** This guesthouse is located in the town of Velas on the island of São Jorge. It has a garden, a terrace, and a shared kitchen. Prices start at \$60 per night.

These are just a few of the many great guesthouses and bed and breakfasts in the Azores. When choosing a guesthouse or bed and breakfast, it is important to consider your budget and your desired location. The Azores have something to offer everyone, so you're sure to find the perfect place to stay.

Here are some additional tips for choosing accommodation in the Azores:
- **Book your accommodation in advance:** The Azores are a popular tourist destination, so it is important to book your accommodation in advance,

especially if you are traveling during the peak season (June-September).

- **Consider your budget:** The Azores have a wide range of accommodation options, from luxury resorts to budget-friendly guesthouses. Decide how much you are willing to spend on accommodation before you start your search.

The guesthouses and bed & breakfasts of the Azores are a window into the islands' soul. Here, you'll find not just a place to lay your head, but an intimate connection to the culture, history, and hospitality that define the archipelago. Whether you seek tranquility, charm, or a glimpse of local life, these accommodations offer an authentic way to experience the Azores' captivating allure.

4.3 Best Self-Catering Apartments and Villas

A Home Away from Home in the Azores

For travelers seeking the freedom to create their own Azorean experience, self-catering apartments and villas provide the perfect solution. Offering a blend of comfort, convenience, and independence, these accommodations allow you to immerse yourself in the islands' beauty while enjoying the comforts of a home away from home.

- **Quinta do Furnas, São Miguel Island:** This villa is located in the Furnas caldera on the island of São Miguel. It has a private pool, a garden, and a barbecue area. Prices start at \$200 per night.
- **Villa Vista do Atlântico, Faial Island:** This villa is located in the town of Horta on the island of Faial. It has a private pool, a terrace, and stunning views of the

Atlantic Ocean. Prices start at \$150 per night.

- **Villa do Porto:** On Santa Maria Island, Villa do Porto offers self-catering villas with modern amenities. With spacious interiors and outdoor spaces, you'll have the freedom to create your ideal vacation. Prices start at around $120 per night, providing a comfortable oasis for families or couples.
- **Casa do Monte, Pico Island:** This apartment is located in the town of Madalena on the island of Pico. It has a balcony with stunning views of the vineyards. Prices start at \$100 per night.
- **Vila da Rosa, Terceira Island:** This villa is located in the town of Angra do Heroísmo on the island of Terceira. It has a garden, a barbecue area, and a shared swimming pool. Prices start at \$120 per night.

- **Apartamento da Tasca, São Jorge Island:** This apartment is located in the town of Velas on the island of São Jorge. It has a balcony with stunning views of the ocean. Prices start at \$80 per night.

These are just a few of the many great self-catering apartments and villas in the Azores. When choosing a self-catering apartment or villa, it is important to consider your budget and your desired location. The Azores have something to offer everyone, so you're sure to find the perfect place to stay.

Here are some additional tips for choosing accommodation in the Azores:

- **Book your accommodation in advance:** The Azores are a popular tourist destination, so it is important to book your accommodation in advance, especially if you are traveling during the peak season (June-September).

- **Consider your budget:** The Azores have a wide range of accommodation options, from luxury resorts to budget-friendly self-catering apartments and villas. Decide how much you are willing to spend on accommodation before you start your search.

Self-catering apartments and villas in the Azores grant you the luxury of crafting your adventure. By blending the comforts of a private residence with the allure of the islands, these accommodations offer a unique way to explore the Azores at your own pace. Whether you're seeking relaxation, a connection with nature, or a taste of local life, these options empower you to make the Azores your own.

4.4 Best Camping and Eco-Lodges

For adventurers who long to be enveloped by the Azores' natural beauty, camping, and eco-lodges provide a unique and eco-conscious way to experience the archipelago. Whether you're pitching a tent amidst breathtaking landscapes or staying in sustainable lodges that harmonize with nature, these accommodations let you embrace the outdoors while treading lightly on the environment.

- **Caparica Azores Ecolodge, Biscoitos:** This eco-lodge is located in the countryside on the island of Terceira. It has a swimming pool, a garden, and a barbecue area. Prices start at \$100 per night.
- **Terra Nostra Eco Park, Furnas:** This eco-park is located in the Furnas caldera on the island of São Miguel. It has a

camping area, a thermal pool, and a variety of hiking trails. Prices start at \$50 per night for camping.

- **Camping do Vulcão, Sete Cidades:** This campsite is located on the rim of the Sete Cidades caldera on the island of São Miguel. It has a swimming pool, a playground, and a barbecue area. Prices start at \$40 per night for camping.
- **Monte Verde Eco-Resort, Faial:** This eco-resort is located in the countryside on the island of Faial. It has a camping area, a swimming pool, and a variety of hiking trails. Prices start at \$60 per night for camping.
- **Gruta do Carvão Eco-Pousada, São Jorge:** This eco-pousada is located in the countryside on the island of São Jorge. It has a swimming pool, a garden, and a barbecue area. Prices start at \$70 per night.

- **Santa Catarina Park Campground:** Nestled on São Miguel Island, Santa Catarina Park Campground offers a prime location for camping enthusiasts. Surrounded by nature and equipped with essential facilities, it's an inviting place to experience the outdoors. Rates start at around $20 per night, offering budget-friendly camping with modern conveniences.

These are just a few of the many great camping and eco-lodges in the Azores. When choosing a camping or eco-lodge, it is important to consider your budget and your desired location. The Azores have something to offer everyone, so you're sure to find the perfect place to stay.

Here are some additional tips for choosing accommodation in the Azores:

- **Book your accommodation in advance:** The Azores are a popular tourist destination, so it is important to

book your accommodation in advance, especially if you are traveling during the peak season (June-September).
- **Consider your budget:** The Azores have a wide range of accommodation options, from luxury resorts to budget-friendly camping and eco-lodges. Decide how much you are willing to spend on accommodation before you start your search.

Camping and eco-lodges in the Azores invite you to disconnect from the everyday and reconnect with nature. Whether you're sleeping under the stars or in sustainable lodges, these accommodations offer a conscious way to experience the archipelago's pristine landscapes. By choosing these options, you not only create unforgettable memories but also contribute to the preservation of the Azores' natural wonders for generations to come.

CHAPTER 5

Transportation in the Azores

5.1 Renting a Car: Exploring the Azores at Your Own Pace

Renting a car is a great way to get around the Azores. The islands are relatively small and have good roads, making it easy to drive between different destinations. Car rentals are also relatively affordable in the Azores.

- **Rent-A-Car Services:** Numerous rent-a-car services are available across the Azores, catering to various preferences and budgets. Both local and international rental companies offer a range of vehicle options, from compact cars to SUVs, ensuring that you find the perfect match for your exploration.

- **Cost Considerations:** Car rental prices in the Azores vary based on factors such as the type of vehicle, rental duration, and the time of year. On average, rental prices for a compact car start at approximately $40 per day. SUVs and larger vehicles may range from $60 to $100 per day, depending on the model and features.
- **Navigating the Islands:** The well-maintained roads of the Azores make navigating the islands a straightforward and enjoyable experience. From winding coastal routes to serene countryside drives, having a rental car allows you to traverse the archipelago's diverse terrain with ease.
- **Island-Hopping Made Easy:** If you're planning to explore multiple islands, renting a car becomes even more convenient. Many rental companies offer

inter-island drop-off options, allowing you to seamlessly transition from one island to another without the hassle of returning the car to its original location.
- **Fuel and Insurance:** It's important to factor in fuel costs and insurance when budgeting for your car rental. Fuel prices in the Azores are reasonable, and rental companies offer various insurance packages to ensure your peace of mind while on the road.

Here are some tips for renting a car in the Azores:
- **Book your car in advance:** The Azores are a popular tourist destination, so it is important to book your car in advance, especially if you are traveling during the peak season (June-September).
- **Compare prices from different rental companies:** There are many different

rental companies operating in the Azores, so it is important to compare prices before you book.

- **Consider the type of car you need:** If you are planning on doing a lot of hiking or exploring the countryside, you will need a car with four-wheel drive.
- **Get insurance:** It is important to get insurance when you rent a car in the Azores. This will protect you in case of an accident or theft.
- **Be aware of the speed limits:** The speed limits in the Azores are lower than in many other countries. Be sure to obey the speed limits to avoid getting a ticket.
- **Be prepared for narrow roads:** The roads in the Azores can be narrow, especially in the countryside. Prepare to drive gently and cautiously.

- **Be aware of the weather:** The weather in the Azores can change quickly. Be prepared for rain, fog, and wind.

Here are some of the best car rental companies in the Azores:

- **Auto Azores:** This company has a wide fleet of cars to choose from, including cars with four-wheel drive.
- **Azorean Rent a Car:** This company is a good option for budget-minded travelers.
- **Mendes Rent a Car:** This company is a good option for travelers who want to rent a luxury car.

Rental car prices in the Azores vary depending on the time of year, the type of car you rent, and the rental company you choose. In general, you can expect to pay between \$50 and \$100 per day for a rental car in the Azores.

Renting a car in the Azores unlocks a world of exploration, granting you the autonomy to uncover the islands' treasures at your leisure. With a range of vehicle options and accessible rental prices, you can embark on a memorable journey that lets you uncover the Azores' natural beauty, cultural richness, and hidden gems with every mile you drive.

5. 2 Public Transportation: Navigating the Azores with Ease

Public transportation in the Azores offers an efficient and budget-friendly way to explore the island's captivating landscapes and vibrant communities. Whether you're island-hopping or exploring a single destination, the well-organized network of buses and ferries ensures that you can embrace the archipelago's charm without the need for a personal vehicle.

- **Bus Services:** Each island boasts an extensive network of bus services that connect major towns, attractions, and points of interest. From São Miguel to Flores, you'll find reliable and punctual buses that offer a comfortable way to traverse the islands.

- **Ferry Connections:** For those looking to hop between islands, the Azores' ferry connections provide a scenic and accessible mode of transportation. Regular ferry services connect several islands, allowing you to explore the archipelago with ease.
- **Cost Considerations:** The cost of public transportation in the Azores is budget-friendly. Bus fares vary by island, with prices starting at approximately $2 for short distances and slightly higher for longer routes. Ferry fares for inter-island travel start at around $20 for passengers, and rates can vary depending on the destination and type of vessel.

- **Advantages of Public Transportation:** Using public transportation offers several advantages, including cost savings and reduced environmental impact. It allows you to focus on the scenery, interact with locals, and immerse yourself in the authentic Azorean experience.
- **Island-Hopping Convenience:** Public transportation facilitates island-hopping by providing connections between ferry ports and bus terminals. Whether you're exploring a new island or returning to your starting point, the transportation network ensures a seamless transition.
- **Local Insights:** Traveling via public transportation allows you to interact with locals, fostering cultural exchange and offering a chance to receive insider tips on the best places to visit, eat, and explore.

- **Timely Information:** The Azores' public transportation system provides accurate and up-to-date schedules, ensuring that you can plan your day's itinerary with confidence.

Here are some tips for using public transportation in the Azores:

- **Plan your route:** The bus schedules in the Azores can be a bit confusing, so it is a good idea to plan your route.
- **Check the bus schedule:** The bus schedules in the Azores can change frequently, so it is important to check the schedule before you travel.
- **Buy a bus pass:** If you are planning on using public transportation a lot, it is a good idea to buy a bus pass. You will save money on individual fares as a result of this.

- **Be patient:** Public transportation in the Azores can be slow, so be patient and enjoy the ride.
- **Be prepared to walk:** In some cases, you may have to walk a short distance to your destination from the bus stop.

Here are the prices for public transportation in the Azores:
- **Bus:** A single bus fare costs \$2.50.
- **Taxi:** A taxi fare starts at \$3.50.

Public transportation in the Azores offers an accessible, affordable, and eco-conscious way to discover the archipelago's myriad treasures. Whether you're wandering through charming towns, admiring stunning landscapes, or embarking on island-hopping adventures, the well-developed network of buses and ferries ensures that you can embrace the Azores' allure while leaving the logistics to the experts.

5. 3 Taxis and Ridesharing: Seamless Mobility in the Azores

When it comes to hassle-free transportation in the Azores, taxis and ridesharing services offer a convenient and comfortable way to navigate the islands. Whether you're looking for a quick ride to your destination or a personalized tour, these options ensure that you can explore the Azores with ease and efficiency.

- **Taxis:** Taxis are readily available on each island, providing a reliable mode of transportation for both short and longer distances. Taxis in the Azores operate using meters, and the initial fare starts at around $4. The per-kilometer rate varies slightly from island to island but generally ranges from $0.40 to $0.60 per kilometer.
- **Ridesharing Services:** Ridesharing services have gained popularity in the

Azores, offering an alternative to traditional taxis. These services, accessible through smartphone apps, provide a convenient way to request a ride and pay digitally.

- **Cost Comparison:** Ridesharing services in the Azores typically have comparable fares to traditional taxis, with slight variations depending on the provider and island. The initial fare for a rideshare service starts at around $4, and the per-kilometer rate is similar to that of taxis, ranging from $0.40 to $0.60 per kilometer.
- **Advantages of Taxis and Ridesharing:** Taxis and ridesharing services offer several benefits, including efficient transportation, local insights from drivers, and the convenience of cashless payments.

- **Personalized Tours:** Both taxis and ridesharing services often provide the option for personalized tours. If you're looking to explore specific attractions or hidden spots, you can negotiate with the driver for a custom itinerary.
- **Airport Transfers:** Taxis and ridesharing services are readily available at airports, providing a seamless transition from your flight to your destination.
- **Local Knowledge:** Drivers in the Azores are often friendly and knowledgeable about the islands' history, culture, and attractions. They can provide valuable insights and recommendations to enhance your travel experience.

Here are some tips for using taxis and ridesharing in the Azores:

Taxis:

- Taxis are metered, and the fare starts at \$3.50.
- Taxis may be hailed on the street or pre-booked.
- Taxis are a good option for short trips and for getting to and from the airport.

Ridesharing:

- Ridesharing services like Uber and Bolt are good options for getting around the city or island.
- The price is computed depending on the distance traveled.
- Ridesharing services can be a cheaper option than taxis, especially for longer trips.

Here are some additional tips for using taxis and ridesharing in the Azores:

- **Be prepared to bargain:** Taxi drivers in the Azores are known for bargaining, so be prepared to negotiate the fare.
- **Know the destination:** Taxi drivers in the Azores may not be familiar with all of the destinations, so it is important to know where you are going before you get in the taxi.
- **Have cash on hand:** Some taxi drivers in the Azores do not accept credit cards, so it is important to have cash on hand.

Taxis and ridesharing services in the Azores offer a straightforward and comfortable way to get around the islands. Whether you're seeking a short ride or a guided tour, these transportation options ensure that you can explore the Azores' beauty and charm while enjoying the convenience of professional and reliable services

CHAPTER 6

Travel Tips for a Memorable Experience

6.1 Respect for Nature and Local Culture

As you embark on your Azorean journey, fostering respect for nature and embracing the local culture is not just etiquette—it's the essence of experiencing the archipelago's magic. From the pristine landscapes to the warm-hearted locals, adopting these values enriches your travels and leaves a positive impact on the Azores.

- **Eco-Friendly Explorations:** While exploring the Azores' natural wonders, be mindful of your impact. Follow designated trails, avoid disturbing wildlife, and refrain from picking plants or leaving litter behind. National parks and protected areas often have entrance fees ranging from $3 to $10, contributing to conservation efforts.

- **Sustainable Accommodations:** Choose environmentally friendly lodgings that have an emphasis on sustainable methods. Many lodges, boutique hotels, and guesthouses in the Azores emphasize responsible tourism and conservation. Prices vary depending on the type of accommodation and location, starting at approximately $70 per night.
- **Cultural Sensitivity:** Engage with locals respectfully, embracing the warmth and traditions that define Azorean culture. Learn a few basic Portuguese phrases—a simple "Bom dia" (good morning) or "Obrigado" (thank you) goes a long way. Immerse yourself in cultural events and festivities, respecting local customs and dress codes.

- **Supporting Local Economy:** When shopping for souvenirs and dining, prioritize local businesses. Not only does this directly contribute to the local economy, but it also provides you with a more authentic and genuine experience. Meals at local restaurants can range from $15 to $40 per person, depending on the establishment and menu.
- **Participating in Guided Tours:** Consider joining guided tours led by knowledgeable locals. These tours often offer insights into the islands' natural history, culture, and conservation efforts. Prices for guided tours vary depending on the duration and type of experience, ranging from $40 to $100 per person.
- **Ethical Wildlife Encounters:** If you're venturing into the ocean for activities like whale watching or swimming with dolphins, choose operators that prioritize

responsible wildlife encounters. These activities typically range from $50 to $100 per person, ensuring that your experience leaves minimal impact on marine life.

- **Giving Back:** Consider participating in volunteer activities that give back to the Azorean community and environment. Whether it's beach cleanups or tree planting, these experiences allow you to leave a positive mark on the islands.

Respect for nature and local culture is the foundation of a truly memorable Azorean adventure. By embracing these values, you not only forge a deeper connection with the archipelago but also play a role in preserving its beauty for generations to come. Your conscious choices,interactions and contribute to the magic that makes the Azores a cherished destination.

6.2 Sustainable Tourism Practices

Embracing sustainable tourism practices in the Azores is not just a choice—it's a responsibility. As you embark on your journey, consider how your choices can preserve the archipelago's natural wonders and cultural richness for generations to come. By adopting sustainable habits, you contribute to a more responsible and rewarding travel experience.

- **Eco-Conscious Accommodations:** Choose accommodations that prioritize sustainable practices. Many lodges, eco-lodges, and guesthouses in the Azores implement energy-saving measures, waste reduction, and local sourcing. Prices for eco-conscious accommodations vary depending on the type of stay and location, starting at approximately $70 per night.

- **Reduce, Reuse, Recycle:** Minimize your environmental impact by adhering to waste management practices. Choose reusable water bottles, reject single-use plastics, and handle trash properly. Most accommodations and public areas in the Azores provide recycling bins for easy disposal.
- **Supporting Local Businesses:** Dine at local restaurants, shop at markets, and support local artisans. By patronizing local businesses, you directly contribute to the Azorean economy while enjoying an authentic experience. Prices for meals at local restaurants range from $15 to $40 per person.
- **Respectful Wildlife Encounters:** When engaging in activities like whale watching or swimming with dolphins, choose operators that prioritize responsible wildlife encounters. Opt for

tours led by experienced guides who respect marine life and adhere to guidelines. Prices for these activities typically range from $50 to $100 per person.

- **Eco-Friendly Transportation:** Opt for eco-friendly transportation options such as public buses or ridesharing services that minimize carbon emissions. Additionally, consider renting hybrid or electric vehicles for your explorations. Rental prices for compact cars start at approximately $40 per day.
- **Participation in Conservation Efforts:** Make a positive impact by participating in local conservation initiatives. Volunteering for beach cleanups, reforestation projects, or wildlife monitoring programs allows you to contribute directly to the Azores' environmental well-being.

- **Responsible Souvenir Choices:** Select souvenirs that align with sustainability principles. Choose locally-made products, artisan crafts, or eco-friendly items that reflect the Azores' culture and beauty.
- **Educate Yourself:** Take the time to learn about the Azores' unique ecosystems, cultural heritage, and conservation efforts. Attend workshops, guided tours, and educational events to deepen your understanding of the archipelago's delicate balance.

Sustainable tourism in the Azores is an investment in the future of the islands. By making thoughtful choices, embracing responsible practices, and nurturing the environment and culture, you leave a positive mark on the archipelago and create memories that resonate beyond your visit.

6.3 Photography Tips: Capturing Azores' Beauty Through Your Lens

The Azores' breathtaking landscapes, vibrant culture, and unique charm offer endless opportunities for stunning photography. To ensure your travel album is a visual masterpiece, follow these photography tips that will help you capture the essence of the Azores and create unforgettable memories.

- **Golden Hour Magic:** Make the most of the magical golden hours just after sunrise and before sunset. The soft, warm light enhances the beauty of the Azorean landscapes, casting a captivating glow on everything you photograph.
- **Weather Adaptability:** The weather in the Azores can be unpredictable. Be prepared for sudden changes by carrying

a waterproof camera bag, lens wipes, and a rain cover for your gear.

- **Wide Angle for Landscapes:** The Azores' landscapes are vast and diverse. Use a wide-angle lens to capture the sweeping vistas, lush greenery, and volcanic wonders in all their grandeur.
- **Details Matter:** Don't forget to zoom in on the intricate details that make the Azores special. From the vibrant tiles of historic buildings to the delicate patterns on flora, capturing these details adds depth to your visual story.
- **Packing Essentials:** Pack extra camera batteries, memory cards, and a tripod. The Azores' natural beauty invites multiple shots, and you wouldn't want to miss a moment due to depleted gear.
- **Cultural Sensitivity:** When photographing locals, especially during events and festivals, be respectful and

ask for permission when appropriate. Engage with the locals to capture candid moments that truly reflect the Azorean way of life.

- **Capture Unique Moments:** Don't hesitate to wake up early or stay out late to capture unique moments, such as the mist rising from the crater lakes during sunrise or the twinkling lights of coastal towns at night.
- **Wildlife Encounters:** If you're lucky to encounter Azores' marine life or bird species, remember to maintain a respectful distance and use a telephoto lens to capture their beauty without disturbing their natural behavior.
- **Editing Magic:** After your adventure, use photo editing software to enhance your images. Adjusting exposure, contrast, and colors can bring out the true

magic of the Azores' landscapes and culture.

The Azores are a photographer's paradise, offering a wealth of captivating subjects to capture. By applying these photography tips, you'll not only create stunning images but also create a visual diary that encapsulates the beauty, culture, and spirit of this enchanting archipelago.

6.4 Unique Souvenirs to Bring Home: Preserving Azorean Memories

Bringing home a piece of the Azores ensures your memories of this enchanting archipelago will last a lifetime. From handmade crafts to culinary delights, the Azores offers an array of unique souvenirs that reflect the islands' culture, natural beauty, and rich history. Here are a few ideas:

- **Azorean Honey:** The Azores are known for their delicious honey, which is made from the nectar of wildflowers that grow on the islands. You can find honey for sale at most grocery stores and souvenir shops in the Azores. Prices start at around €5 for a small jar.
- **Terra Nostra Botanical Garden Coffee Mug:** The Terra Nostra Botanical Garden is one of the most popular tourist attractions in the Azores. It is home to a variety of exotic plants and flowers, as well as a thermal pool. You can buy a coffee mug with the Terra Nostra logo on it at the garden's gift shop. Prices start at around €10.
- **Blue Azorean Wool Sweater:** The Azores are known for their blue wool sweaters, which are made from a type of wool that is unique to the islands. These sweaters are warm and stylish, and they

make a great souvenir to bring home from your trip. Prices start at around €50 for a basic sweater.

- **Pico Island Wine:** Pico Island is known for its delicious wine, which is made from the Verdelho grape. You can find Pico Island wine for sale at most grocery stores and souvenir shops in the Azores. Prices start at around €10 for a bottle.
- **Azorean Music Box:** The Azores have a rich musical heritage, and you can find a variety of beautiful music boxes for sale on the islands. These music boxes are a great way to bring a little bit of the Azores home with you. Prices start at around €20 for a small music box.
- **Traditional Azorean Pottery:** Handcrafted pottery, adorned with intricate designs and vibrant colors, is a hallmark of Azorean artistry. Pieces such as decorative tiles, bowls, and vases

capture the essence of the islands. Prices for pottery items start at approximately $10, depending on the size and intricacy of the piece.

- **Embroidered Linens:** Azorean embroidery is a cherished tradition passed down through generations. Intricately stitched linens, from tablecloths to handkerchiefs, showcase the skill and creativity of local artisans. Prices for embroidered linens vary based on size and complexity, starting at around $20.
- **São Jorge Cheese:** Renowned around the world, São Jorge cheese is a must-bring souvenir. This distinct cow's milk cheese boasts a tangy flavor and crumbly texture. You can purchase wheels of São Jorge cheese at local markets, with prices ranging from $10 to $20, depending on size and quality.

- **Traditional Handicrafts:** Exploring local markets reveals an array of traditional handicrafts, including woven baskets, wooden utensils, and woolen items. These crafts showcase the islanders' creativity and commitment to preserving their heritage. Prices for handicrafts start at approximately $10.
- **Tea and Pineapple Delights:** Azores is known for its tea plantations and pineapple cultivation. Tea leaves and pineapple products, such as jams and liqueurs, make for delectable and unique gifts. Tea packages start at around $5, while pineapple products range from $5 to $15.
- **Whale-Themed Keepsakes:** As a nod to the Azores' strong connection with the ocean and its marine life, consider bringing home whale-themed souvenirs. Items such as artistic prints, jewelry, and

ornaments capture the beauty of these majestic creatures. Prices vary based on the item and craftsmanship.

Here are some additional tips for buying souvenirs in the Azores:
- **Negotiate:** Don't be scared to haggle with store owners. They are often willing to give you a discount if you ask.
- **Buy from local businesses:** When you buy souvenirs from local businesses, you are helping to support the local economy.
- **Pack your souvenirs carefully:** The Azores are known for their strong winds, so it is important to pack your souvenirs carefully so that they don't break in transit.

Souvenirs from the Azores are not just tokens—they're cherished memories encapsulating the islands' spirit. Whether you choose handcrafted pottery, exquisite embroidery, or delectable treats, each souvenir tells a story of your journey through the Azores. By supporting local artisans and businesses, you not only bring home treasures but also contribute to the preservation of the archipelago's culture and traditions.

CHAPTER 7

Practical Information

7.1 Emergency Contacts: Your Safety Net in the Azores

While the Azores are a paradise of natural beauty and cultural richness, it's important to be prepared for any unforeseen situations. Familiarizing yourself with emergency contacts ensures you have a safety net should you need assistance during your travels in this captivating archipelago.

- **Emergency Services:** In case of immediate danger or emergencies, dial 112. This universal emergency number connects you to police, medical assistance, and firefighters. It's crucial to keep this number handy at all times.

- **Medical Assistance:** If you require medical attention, Azores has a network of health centers and hospitals across its islands. For non-urgent medical concerns, contact your accommodations for recommendations or directions to the nearest facility. Consultations with general practitioners typically start at around $50, depending on the complexity of the case.
- **Pharmacies:** Pharmacies are well-distributed across the Azores. Look for the sign "Farmácia" to locate one. They provide over-the-counter medications, health advice, and prescriptions. Medicine prices vary based on the type and brand, with common pain relievers costing around $5 to $10.
- **Police Assistance:** If you encounter any safety concerns or require police

assistance that is not an immediate emergency, dial 112 for general emergencies or visit the nearest police station. The police are generally approachable and can offer assistance in various situations.

- **Lost or Stolen Documents:** In the unfortunate event of losing your passport, identification, or other important documents, contact your country's embassy or consulate. They can guide the steps to take for replacement. Remember to keep copies of your important documents, such as your passport, separately from the originals.
- **Embassy Contacts:** For travelers from the United States, the U.S. Embassy in Lisbon can assist. Contact them at +351 21 770 2122. Travelers from other countries should note the contact details

of their respective embassies or consulates in Portugal.

- **Travel Insurance:** Having comprehensive travel insurance is essential. It covers medical expenses, trip cancellations, and other unforeseen incidents. Prices for travel insurance vary depending on coverage and duration, starting at approximately $30 for a week-long trip.

Here is the list of some emergency contacts that you may need while in the Azores:

- **Medical emergency:** 112
- **Fire department:** 112
- **Police:** 112
- **Roadside assistance:** 808 208 080
- **Tourist information:** 296 284 070

Emergency number 112 is the number to call for all emergencies in the Azores. It is free to call from any landline or mobile phone.

The cost of calling the emergency number 112 from a mobile phone varies depending on your phone plan. However, it is usually covered by your insurance.

Here are some additional tips for staying safe in the Azores:
- **Be aware of your surroundings:** Be mindful of your surroundings and take precautions to stay safe, especially at night.
- **Don't leave valuables unattended:** Don't leave your valuables unattended, even for a few minutes.
- **Be careful when driving:** The roads in the Azores can be narrow and winding, so be careful when driving.
- **Be prepared for bad weather:** The Azores are known for their unpredictable weather, so be prepared for rain, wind, and fog.

Though the Azores are generally safe, it's wise to be prepared for any situation. Equipping yourself with emergency contacts and ensuring you have the necessary insurance safeguards your travel experience. By having this information on hand, you can navigate any challenges with confidence, knowing that help is just a phone call away.

7.2 Health and Medical Services: Your Well-being in the Azores

Prioritizing your health while traveling in the Azores ensures a worry-free and enjoyable experience. Familiarizing yourself with available health and medical services, as well as associated costs, offers peace of mind as you explore this captivating archipelago.

- **The National Health Service (Serviço Nacional de Saúde, SNS):** The SNS is the public healthcare system in Portugal. It is free for Portuguese citizens and residents, but there may be a charge for some services. Visitors to the Azores from other EU countries are also entitled to free healthcare under the SNS, but they may need to show their European Health Insurance Card (EHIC). Visitors from non-EU countries will need to pay for healthcare, and prices can be high.
- **Private hospitals and clinics:** There are also many private hospitals and clinics in the Azores. These hospitals offer a wider range of services than the SNS hospitals, and they may be more convenient for visitors who do not speak Portuguese. However, prices at private hospitals are much higher than at SNS hospitals.

- **Pharmacies:** Pharmacies, denoted by the sign "Farmácia," are well-distributed across the islands. They offer over-the-counter medications, health advice, and prescription services. The prices of medicines vary based on type and brand, with common pain relievers costing around $5 to $10.
- **Health Insurance:** It's highly recommended to have comprehensive travel health insurance that covers medical expenses during your stay. This insurance provides financial security in case of unexpected health issues. Prices for travel insurance vary depending on coverage and duration, starting at approximately $30 for a week-long trip.
- **Emergency care:** In the event of a medical emergency, you should call 112. This is the emergency number for all of

Portugal, and it is free to call from any landline or mobile phone.

- **Doctors:** If you need to see a doctor, you can either go to an SNS health center or a private clinic. To see a doctor at a SNS health center, you will need to make an appointment. You can make an appointment by calling the health center or by going online. To see a doctor at a private clinic, you do not need to make an appointment. However, you may have to wait longer to see a doctor.
- **Hospitals:** If you need to go to the hospital, you can go to a SNS hospital or a private hospital. If you go to a SNS hospital, you will need to bring your EHIC card or proof of payment. If you go to a private hospital, you will need to pay for your treatment upfront.
- **Vaccinations and Precautions:** Ensure you're up to date with routine

vaccinations before traveling to the Azores. If you have specific health concerns, consult your healthcare provider about recommended vaccinations or precautions.

- **Prescriptions:** If your doctor prescribes medication, you can either get it filled at a SNS pharmacy or a private pharmacy. To get your medication filled at a SNS pharmacy, you will need to bring your prescription and your EHIC card or proof of payment. To get your medication filled at a private pharmacy, you will need to pay for your medication upfront.

Here are some additional tips for staying healthy in the Azores:

- **Drink plenty of fluids:** The Azores can be hot and humid, so it is important to drink plenty of fluids to stay hydrated.

- **Use sunscreen:** The sun in the Azores can be strong, so it is important to use sunscreen to protect your skin.
- **Cover-up:** If you are going to be spending time in the sun, it is a good idea to cover up with long sleeves and pants.
- **Eat healthy foods:** Eating healthy foods will help to boost your immune system and keep you healthy.
- **Get a lot of sleep:** Getting a lot of sleep is important for your overall health and well-being.

Taking care of your health while in the Azores is essential for a seamless and enjoyable trip. By being prepared with the necessary health information and insurance coverage, you can explore the islands with confidence, knowing that your well-being is a priority.

7.3 Internet and Connectivity: Staying Connected in the Azores

In an increasingly digital world, staying connected while traveling is crucial. The Azores offer a range of options for internet and connectivity, ensuring you can share your experiences, stay in touch, and access essential information throughout your journey.

- **Mobile Data and SIM Cards:** Most major mobile carriers offer coverage in the Azores. If you have an unlocked smartphone, consider purchasing a local SIM card upon arrival. This allows you to have a local number and access to data plans for browsing and communication. Prices for SIM cards and data packages vary based on the provider and package, starting at approximately $10.

- **Wi-Fi Availability:** Wi-Fi is widely available in hotels, restaurants, cafes, and public spaces across the Azores. While exploring towns and cities, you'll find plenty of establishments offering complimentary Wi-Fi, making it easy to stay connected on the go.
- **Internet Cafes:** Internet cafes are not as common in the Azores as they once were, given the prevalence of mobile data and Wi-Fi. However, in larger towns and tourist areas, you may still find internet cafes where you can use computers and access the internet for a fee.
- **Coverage and Connectivity:** Urban areas and popular tourist spots in the Azores generally have good network coverage, ensuring you can make calls, send messages, and browse the internet without major interruptions. In more

remote and rural areas, coverage might be less consistent.

- **Digital Maps and Navigation:** Offline map apps such as Google Maps can be a valuable tool for navigating the Azores. Download the maps and directions while connected to Wi-Fi to ensure you can access them even if you're in an area with limited connectivity.
- **Roaming Charges:** If you plan to use your home mobile plan while in the Azores, be aware of potential roaming charges. Contact your mobile carrier before your trip to understand the costs and options for using your phone abroad.
- **Public Wi-Fi Safety:** When using public Wi-Fi, exercise caution when accessing sensitive information, such as online banking or entering passwords. To improve security, consider adopting a virtual private network (VPN).

Here are some additional tips for staying connected in the Azores:

- **Get a local SIM card:** If you plan on using your phone for internet access while you are in the Azores, it is a good idea to get a local SIM card. You will save money on roaming expenses.
- **Use public wifi wisely:** Public wifi can be less secure than your home wifi. Be careful about what information you share when you are using public wifi.
- **Download maps and apps offline:** If you are planning on doing a lot of hiking or exploring in the Azores, it is a good idea to download maps and apps offline. This will save your data and allow you to use your phone even when you don't have cell reception.

Staying connected in the Azores is both convenient and achievable. With options like local SIM cards, widespread Wi-Fi availability, and reliable network coverage, you can share your adventures, access information, and communicate with ease while immersing yourself in the archipelago's beauty and culture.

7.4 Important Local Customs and Etiquette: Navigating Azorean Culture with Respect

Immersing yourself in the local culture of the Azores goes beyond admiring the landscapes—it involves understanding and respecting the customs and etiquette that shape the lives of its warm-hearted inhabitants. By familiarizing yourself with these practices, you'll forge genuine connections and create meaningful experiences during your journey.

- **Greetings:** When greeting someone in the Azores, it is customary to shake hands. Men greet men and women greet women. If you are close friends with someone, you may also give them a hug or two kisses on the cheek.

- **Dining etiquette:** When dining in the Azores, it is customary to wait for everyone to be seated before starting to eat. It is also customary to leave a small amount of food on your plate as a sign that you have enjoyed the meal.
- **Tipping:** Tipping is not expected in the Azores, but it is appreciated. A small tip of around 10% is considered appropriate.
- **Photography:** It is generally considered polite to ask permission before taking someone's photo. This is especially important when taking photos of people in religious or cultural settings.
- **Public displays of affection:** Public displays of affection are not common in

the Azores. It is best to avoid hugging, kissing, or holding hands in public.

- **Clothing:** The Azores have a mild climate, so you can usually get away with wearing casual clothing. However, it is a good idea to pack a light jacket for evenings and cooler weather. It is also a good idea to dress respectfully when visiting religious or cultural sites.
- **Respecting Personal Space:** Azoreans value personal space, so it's important to maintain a comfortable distance when interacting. A respectful and friendly demeanor is always appreciated.
- **Attending Religious Ceremonies:** If you're attending a religious ceremony, dress modestly and observe quietly and respectfully. Always follow the lead of the locals present.
- **Polite language:** It is important to use polite language when speaking to people

in the Azores. This includes using the formal "você" instead of the informal "tu" when addressing someone you don't know well.

By embracing these local customs and etiquette, you'll not only deepen your connection with the Azores but also enrich your experiences and interactions. Showing respect for the traditions and values of this beautiful archipelago will not only enhance your trip but also leave a positive impression on the locals you meet along the way.

CHAPTER 8

Azores Travel Itinerary Suggestions

8.1 One-Week Itinerary

I recently had the pleasure of exploring the Azores, and I can confidently say that this archipelago is a true gem. With its stunning landscapes, rich culture, and fascinating history, there is something for everyone to enjoy.

If you're planning a trip to the Azores, I highly recommend following this one-week itinerary. It will take you to some of the most iconic destinations in the region, providing a well-rounded exploration of this enchanting corner of the world. I guarantee you'll have a memorable journey that you'll cherish for years to come!

- **Day 1:** Arrive in Ponta Delgada, the capital of São Miguel Island. After checking into your accommodation, spend the day visiting the city. In the evening, enjoy a traditional Azorean meal at a local restaurant.
- **Day 2:** Take a day trip to Sete Cidades, a volcanic crater lake located in the western part of São Miguel Island. Hike around the lake and visit the Sete Cidades village. In the evening, go whale watching off the coast of São Miguel Island.
- **Day 3:** Visit the Terra Nostra Botanical Garden, a beautiful garden located in Furnas. Take a dip in the thermal pools and enjoy the natural beauty of the garden. In the evening, have dinner at a restaurant in Furnas and try some of the

local specialties, such as cozido das furnas, a stew cooked in the ground.
- **Day 4:** Hike to the top of the Fogo Volcano, the highest point on São Miguel Island. The journey is difficult but rewarding, and the views from the summit are breathtaking. In the evening, enjoy a barbecue dinner at a restaurant in the Ribeira Grande area.
- **Day 5:** Take a ferry to the island of Faial. Explore the town of Horta, known for its colorful houses and its historic harbor. In the evening, enjoy a drink at Peter's Cafe Sport, a famous bar in Horta.
- **Day 6:** Visit the Capelinhos Volcano, an active volcano that erupted in 1957. The eruption destroyed the village of Capelinhos, but the new landscape is now a popular tourist destination. In the evening, enjoy a traditional Azorean dinner at a restaurant in Horta.

- **Day 7:** Relax on the beach in Furnas or Ponta Delgada before your departure.

This is simply a recommended schedule; you may tailor it to your own interests and time limitations.. The Azores are a beautiful archipelago with something to offer everyone, so whatever you choose to do, you will have a terrific time.

This one-week itinerary offers a taste of the Azores' diverse landscapes, rich culture, and unforgettable experiences. While there's much more to explore in the archipelago, this journey provides a well-rounded introduction to the beauty and charm that the Azores have to offer.

8.2 Two-Week Itinerary: A Deep Dive into Azorean Beauty and Culture

For those seeking a more immersive exploration of the Azores, a two-week itinerary allows you to delve deeper into the archipelago's diverse landscapes, cultural treasures, and hidden gems. This itinerary offers a comprehensive journey through the Azores' captivating islands, providing a truly unforgettable experience.

- **Day 1:** Arrive in Ponta Delgada, the capital of São Miguel Island. After checking into your accommodation, spend the day visiting the city. In the evening, enjoy a traditional Azorean meal at a local restaurant.
- **Day 2:** Take a day trip to Sete Cidades, a volcanic crater lake located in the western part of São Miguel Island. Hike

around the lake and visit the Sete Cidades village. In the evening, go whale watching off the coast of São Miguel Island.

- **Day 3:** Visit the Terra Nostra Botanical Garden, a beautiful garden located in Furnas. Take a dip in the thermal pools and enjoy the natural beauty of the garden. In the evening, have dinner at a restaurant in Furnas and try some of the local specialties, such as cozido das furnas, a stew cooked in the ground.
- **Day 4:** Hike to the top of the Fogo Volcano, the highest point on São Miguel Island. The journey is difficult but rewarding, and the views from the summit are breathtaking. In the evening, enjoy a barbecue dinner at a restaurant in the Ribeira Grande area.
- **Day 5:** Take a ferry to the island of Faial. Explore the town of Horta, known for its

colorful houses and its historic harbor. In the evening, enjoy a drink at Peter's Cafe Sport, a famous bar in Horta.

- **Day 6:** Visit the Capelinhos Volcano, an active volcano that erupted in 1957. The eruption destroyed the village of Capelinhos, but the new landscape is now a popular tourist destination. In the evening, enjoy a traditional Azorean dinner at a restaurant in Horta.
- **Day 7:** Take a ferry to the island of Pico. Visit the Pico Island Wine Company and learn about the production of Pico Island wine, one of the most famous wines in Portugal. In the evening, visit a local vineyard for a wine tasting.
- **Day 8:** Hike to the top of Mount Pico, the highest mountain in Portugal. The journey is difficult but rewarding, and the views from the summit are breathtaking. In the evening, enjoy a

traditional Azorean dinner at a restaurant in Madalena.
- **Day 9:** Take a ferry to the island of Terceira. Visit the Angra do Heroísmo, a UNESCO World Heritage Site. In the evening, enjoy a traditional Azorean dinner at a restaurant in Angra do Heroísmo.
- **Day 10:** Visit the Algar do Carvão, a lava cave located on Terceira Island. Learn about the cave's history by taking a guided tour. In the evening, enjoy a traditional Azorean dinner at a restaurant in Biscoitos.
- **Day 11:** Take a ferry to the island of São Jorge. Visit the Fajã dos Cubres, a small village located on a cliff. In the evening, enjoy a traditional Azorean dinner at a restaurant in Velas.
- **Day 12:** Hike to the top of the Velas Volcano, the highest point on São Jorge

Island. The journey is difficult but rewarding, and the views from the summit are breathtaking. In the evening, enjoy a traditional Azorean dinner at a restaurant in Velas.

- **Day 13:** Take a ferry back to Ponta Delgada, São Miguel Island. Relax on the beach or explore the city before your departure.

This is simply a recommended schedule; you may tailor it to your interests and time limitations. The Azores are a beautiful archipelago with something to offer everyone.

A two-week itinerary allows you to fully immerse yourself in the Azores' wonders, from its dramatic landscapes to its rich culture and history. Each island offers a unique experience, ensuring that your journey through this enchanting archipelago is nothing short of unforgettable.

Conclusion

Embark on Your Azorean Odyssey

As you close the final pages of this Azores travel guide, you're not just concluding a book—you're embarking on a journey of your own. The Azores, with their breathtaking landscapes, vibrant culture, and captivating history, have beckoned to you from these pages, inviting you to experience their wonders firsthand.

From the lush crater lakes of São Miguel to the rugged cliffs of São Jorge, each island offers a unique tapestry of natural beauty and local charm. The Azores' authenticity lies not only in its stunning vistas but in the warm smiles of its people, the taste of traditional dishes, and the echoes of centuries-old traditions.

As you traverse volcanic landscapes, navigate through historic streets, and immerse yourself in the tranquil rhythm of island life, remember that the Azores offer more than just a vacation—they offer a transformative experience. Let the stunning vistas and diverse adventures remind you that the world is full of surprises, waiting to be discovered.

Whether you seek adrenaline-pumping activities, serene moments in nature, or the joy of connecting with locals, the Azores provide the canvas on which to paint your own stories and memories. So pack your bags, embrace the unknown, and set forth on your Azorean odyssey. Go embrace these captivating islands, your journey will be filled with wonder, discovery, and the realization that the Azores will forever hold a special place in your heart.

Bon voyage, intrepid traveler. Your Azorean adventure awaits.

Printed in Great Britain
by Amazon

42001111R00149